Praise for *G*

Mark Kuhne's book sets hungry believers—
a sea alive with abundant possibilities that
the energy from your storms of adversity to
an entirely new way. As he shares his story,
veil of your sunglasses, find the keys to transformation, and break through.
book builds your faith and gives you power to spiritually grow. Not only will you will discover
the purpose behind your storms; with God as your Captain, you will learn to navigate the
roughest of seas.

—**Brian Klemmer,** Klemmer & Associates,
international consultant, speaker, and bestselling author
of *The Compassionate Samurai, If How To's were Enough We'd*
All Be Skinny, Rich and Happy, and many others.

I was honored when Mark asked me to read his manuscript Giving God the Helm:
Overcoming Storms of Adversity. *This book is God-inspired and Mark has been led*
by the Holy Spirit as He walked with Mark throughout every page even before he even put
pen to paper. Mark thought he was sending the manuscript to me just for an endorsement, but
what he didn't know is that God knew I needed to read it, NOW! The Apostle Paul said in
2 Timothy 4:2, "...be ready in season and out of season..." to tell others what He has done
for you. This book is Mark's testimony about the lousy captain he was of his life, but what an
incredible Captain we have in Jesus. You cannot put a dollar value on Mark's testimony and
transformed life as he yielded himself entirely to the Master Mariner. Please invest in your
future and buy this book, then read it, then apply what you have read.

—**Nigel Allan,** international sales trainer, conference
speaker, evangelist, and author of *The Key to Life* and
Mastering Incoming Sales Calls.

It is an honor and privilege to endorse this book for Mark Kuhne. The very title, "Giving
God the Helm, Overcoming Storms of Adversity," suggests victory and how to live the life
of an overcomer! It is a prophetic book, in that it comes at the time when so many today
are discouraged, discontent and desperate for change in the midst of adversity. Mark, like
a number of artists, has his own style of painting and writing. This book is an easy read
and is filled with inspiring words of life, which will challenge you to reach the top of the
mountains of life and soar like an eagle above and through the storms of adversity.

—**Prophet Benjamin Smith,** founder, Elisha Company
of Prophets Inc. and Kingdom Community Center Inc.

Through the centuries, truths and lessons have been passed from one generation to the next through the telling of stories. In this book, Mark Kuhne takes us on a gripping journey that demonstrates that storms of adversity in your life can prepare you for so much more. Life happens, and with it come trials. Mark demonstrates how by a renewed mind and renovated thinking you can create new routines that will help you obtain your goals. Stop drifting aimlessly. Don't let your circumstances shipwreck you. Learn how to grasp onto the power and abilities God has given you.

> —**Tracy Trost,** co-writer and director at Trost Moving Pictures independent film studio, in the business of telling great stories and making waves in the entertainment arena, including the multi-award winning film *Find Me*, the nationally released film *A Christmas Snow*, and *The Lamp* based on a book by best-selling author Jim Stovall (set for release in spring 2011)

Yes, whether they originally intended to or not, there are people out there who entice "good" people into ill winds. Using God's Holy Word, Mark articulates exactly what you need to know to survive storms of adversities in your life. Read and receive new understanding of how you can recognize the things and people in life that lead to tumultuous life experiences, which can be so easily avoided with the wisdom and understanding Mark shares with all of us.

> —**Timothy Peterson**, DMin, senior pastor, Christ Family Church International and Christian Family Church World Outreach.

Thank you for reliving this pain in your past so others can learn from your experiences and avoid raging waters bearing down on their souls! Giving God the Helm, Overcoming Storms of Adversity *will be in my self-helps reach for all those who need to be ready to identify the unreasonable people and situations in life.*

> —**Cherrié Peterson**, pastor, counselor, Christ Family Church International and Christian Family Church World Outreach.

Giving God the Helm

Overcoming Storms of Adversity

Giving God the Helm

Overcoming Storms of Adversity

Mark Kuhne

Overcoming For Life LLC

Since 2010

© 2011 by Mark Kuhne
All rights reserved
Printed in the United States of America

ISBN: 978-0-615-42903-8

Published by Overcoming For Life LLC, Mark Kuhne, c/o Koepke Law
Group, 3161 Fernbrook Lane N, Minneapolis, MN, 55447,
www.OvercomingForLife.com, e-mail info@OvercomingForLife.com, fax
(877) 569-6142, phone (612) 518-6516.

First Printing 2011
In the U.S. write:
        Mark Kuhne
        6106 Birch Road, Prior Lake, MN, 55372
        info@OvercomingForLife.com
        www.OvercomingForLife.com

OVERCOMING FOR LIFE

The Overcoming For Life logo is a trademark of Overcoming For Life LLC.

This publication is designed to provide accurate and authoritative
information with regard to the subject matter covered. It is provided with the
understanding that the publisher is not engaged in rendering legal, accounting,
or other professional advice. If legal advice or other expert professional
assistance is required, the services of a competent professional person should
be sought.

> —from a Declaration of Principals jointly adopted
> by a Committee of the American Bar Association
> and a Committee of Publishers & Associations

Slow Fade
© 2007 Sony/ATV Music Publishing LLC and My Refuge Music. All rights
on behalf of Sony/ATV Music Publishing LLC administered by Sony/ATV
Music Publishing LLC, 8 Music Square West, Nashville, TN 37203. All rights
reserved. Used by permission.
Sony/ATV Music Publishing LLC percent control: 25%

Song ID: 42842
Song Title: *Slow Fade*
Writer(s): Mark Hall
Label Copy:
Copyright © 2007 My Refuge Music (BMI) (adm. at EMICMGPublishing. com)/Club Zoo Music (BMI)/SWECS Music (BMI) All rights reserved. Used by permission.
EMI CMG percent control: 75%

Paintings by Mark Kuhne are copyrighted. All rights are reserved.

Except for Bible characters, all characters, names, places, and details used in *Giving God the Helm: Overcoming Storms of Adversities* (in the anecdotes, whether online, in print, or in any other media) are fictitious or have been changed to protect privacy or to invoke Bible stories. Any similarity to real people is a coincidence.

All trade names, product names, painting titles, and trademarks of third parties are the registered and unregistered marks of their respective owners. Any trademarks, logos, and service marks not owned on behalf of Overcoming For Life LLC and/or Mark Kuhne and that are displayed on the www. OvercomingForLife.com web site in photographic form are the registered and unregistered marks of their respective owners. No sponsorship, endorsement, or affiliation by or with those third parties exists or should be implied.

This story of an experience with a pontoon boat (as well as the other stories, dreams, and experiences) is a wonderful metaphor and provides humor to lessons that are not funny at all. Laughter helps cure the soul. Further, our fight is not against flesh and blood:

For we do not wrestle against flesh and blood, but against principalities, against powers, against the rulers of the darkness of this age, against spiritual hosts of wickedness in the heavenly places.

Ephesians 6:12

All Scripture quotations, unless otherwise indicated, are taken from the New King James Version®. Copyright ©1982 by Thomas Nelson, Inc. Used by permission, all rights reserved.

I dedicate this book to my wife Kristin, my children, family, and friends who have stood by me through our circumstances with patience and understanding. May their sacrifices be seed into the Kingdom of God. I ask you Lord to open the windows of Heaven and shower them with blessings. I ask you Lord to bring increase to their fields and that their harvest is bountiful. May they serve you, Lord, with all that they have and all that they are to edify the body of Christ.

...for all have sinned and fall short of the glory of God, being justified freely by His grace through the redemption that is in Christ Jesus...

Romans 3:23–24

In Him you also trusted, after you heard the word of truth, the gospel of your salvation; in whom also, having believed, you were sealed with the Holy Spirit of promise, who is the guarantee of our inheritance until the redemption of the purchased possession, to the praise of His glory.

Ephesians 1:13–14

Contents

Acknowledgements   x

Foreword   xi

Introduction   15

Prologue: The Parable of the Pontoon Boat   20

Chapter 1: Attracted by the Lure   28

Chapter 2: Taking the Bait   47

Chapter 3: Casting Off on the Voyage   64

Chapter 4: Navigating Badly   86

Chapter 5: Beset by Ill Winds   97

Chapter 6: Changing Direction   112

Chapter 7: Battling the Storm   122

Chapter 8: The Storm Worsens   129

Chapter 9: Am I Sinking, Lord?   143

Chapter 10: Assessing Damage from the Storm   153

Chapter 11: Steady as You Go!   159

Chapter 12: God the Gracious Captain   185

Afterword   195

Bible Verse Affirmations   197

Additional Resources   208

About the Author   213

About the Overcoming For Life Logo   218

Acknowledgments

Thank you

—Pastors Timothy Peterson, Doctorate of Ministry, and Cherrié Peterson who feed me hope, wisdom, and understanding. Many of their messages from the pulpit helped me overcome my storms of adversities but were too numerous to record in the Resources section. This book *Giving God the Helm* would not have been possible had they not encouraged me to write my story.

—Jean Cook, principal of editorial services at ImageSmythe, who edited the manuscript, for her wonderful ideas and organizational skills. She was instrumental in helping me complete this book; Jean pushed me to write much more about my story after she reviewed my first draft.

—Kevin Koepke, Koepke Law Group, who helped me understand my story. More than he may know, his gracious support helped changed my perspective tremendously.

—Caitlin Kuhne, who provided graphic design and layout advice and helped with imaging.

—and last but not least, the love of my life, my wife and best friend Kristin, who, despite my faults, has never ceased loving and supporting me and our vision. I cannot image life without her.

Foreword

Now the serpent was more cunning than any beast of the field which the LORD God had made. And he said to the woman, "Has God indeed said, 'You shall not eat of every tree of the garden'?"

Genesis 3:1

Well, if you are ever offered something for free, you might want to think again and ask yourself, "Is it really free?" In *Giving God the Helm: Overcoming Storms of Adversity*, Mark Kuhne knocks the ball out of the park. I have been hoping someone would write this book, and here it is. If you are at all active in this game we call life, this book is a must-read. Sooner or later—assuming it's not already too late—you need to know what's in this book.

Several years ago I had a similar situation to Mark's in which I was offered an opportunity to buy a multimillion-dollar building for our ministry. They told me "not to worry" and "they would take care of everything." They even said they were "told by God that it was their calling to pay for this particular project for our ministry." Need I say anything more? It wasn't free. They walked out on me after only a few months of financial support. I was left paying on a multimillion dollar mortgage all by myself.

In my teaching series "Storm Survivors," I used one of Jesus' parables in the gospel of Matthew in which Jesus taught his disciples the difference between wise and foolish people:

> *"Therefore whoever hears these sayings of Mine, and does them, I will liken him to a wise man who built his house on the rock: and the rain descended, the floods came, and the winds blew and beat on that house; and it did not fall, for it was founded on the rock. But everyone who hears these sayings of Mine, and does not do them, will be like a foolish man who built his house on the sand: and the rain descended, the floods came, and the winds blew and beat on that house; and it fell. And great was its fall."*
>
> **Matthew 7:24–27**

The parable depicts two kinds of people, wise people and foolish people. Whether you are wise or foolish, Jesus wanted us to know that adversity is part of life. The most important message Jesus gave in the parable, however, is why the first man—the wise man—persevered and achieved victory over his adversities, and the second man—the foolish man—experienced great ruin. What made the difference? Simply this, the wise man built his life on the sayings of Christ, the Word of God. The foolish man did not.

In my situation, I was fortunate that God delivered me by sending a buyer for our ministry property before I was forced to turn the property back over to the bank. Interestingly enough, *I really learned my lesson* the day we sold that property. Leaving the lawyers office that grand and glorious day, the Holy Spirit in a still small voice said, "We have been delivered from wicked and unreasonable men." *Wicked and unreasonable men?* Yes, similar to the ones you're going to read about in Mark's book. And, similar to the ones the apostle Paul speaks of as follows:

Finally, brethren, pray for us, that the word of the Lord may run swiftly and be glorified, just as it is with you, and that we may be delivered from unreasonable and wicked men; for not all have faith. But the Lord is faithful, who will establish you and guard you from the evil one.

2 Thessalonians 3:1–3

Yes, whether they originally intended to or not, there are people out there who entice "good" people into ill winds. Using God's Holy Word, Mark articulates exactly what you need to know to survive storms of adversities in your life. Read and receive new understanding of how you can recognize the things and people in life that lead to tumultuous life experiences, which can be so easily avoided with the wisdom and understanding Mark shares with all of us.

—Timothy Peterson, DMin, senior pastor,
Christ Family Church International,
Christian Family Church World Outreach

Introduction

What difficulties are you facing? What tumultuous sea is tossing you to and fro? When a person's spirit is broken, the person loses hope (see Proverbs 18:14). Maybe like me, you have considered giving up hope. The adversities you face are bigger than you think you and your strength can bear. Maybe the waves are pouring in your boat faster than you can bail the water out. I've also faced such waves—maybe we shared the same boat! I found my way to safer waters by relying on God and not my own strength. I had been following God—but this time I actually gave God the helm.

Writing this book was difficult because, although I believe the most threatening storm I describe in these pages is behind me, I would prefer never to journey there again. On the other hand, if you can avoid terrible circumstances because of my experiences, then it is worth every moment in writing this book. You will learn more about my battle, how the Lord gave me warnings, and how the Lord helped and guided me. What should we learn to help keep waves of trouble at bay? How can we recognize trouble when it comes in a beautiful package that looks like a "blessing"? What part of my character was vulnerable? What part of my armor was weak? Why was I so discerning in some ways and so gullible in others? If this weakness is a permanent part of my character, then what additional armor could I employ to help me in the future?

What part of your character has created undesirable circumstances for you? What weaknesses do you have in your armor? Are you ready to journey with me as we find out more about circumstances and how to use them to grow stronger? Maybe you are not quite sure about giving the helm over to God, yet you want to know more. As you read, you may want to laugh or cry with me—or at me. Go ahead. You will learn soon enough that I laugh at myself. You will learn that my wife and shipmate Kristin laughs at me too! To be fair, she also had plenty of tears and anguish through these circumstances. You will learn how my wife, my best friend, stood by me and supported me.

> **Life's trials and tribulations are very much like mighty waves bearing down on our souls.**

Life's trials and tribulations are very much like mighty waves bearing down on our souls. Some of you may be sinking and wondering when the Coast Guard is going to show up and throw you a float or life ring. Others need to make changes to your course headings to navigate seas and winds if you wish to see your destination anytime soon. Bearings and headings are limitless! See your Captain for details.

It isn't easy to hand over the helm to the Captain when you do not readily see him in the boat. Could it be that the Captain was there but I was blinded by circumstances, by the sun, by water spraying into my eyes? Perhaps my eyes were clouded by the gray skies with little light to guide me? What did my perception of my circumstances have to do with the reality that dangerous waves were breaking over the gunwales? What kind of journey am I on? No doubt, the journey was testing me! The open sea is a wilderness that isn't for the weak or naive. You may have sleepless nights and cry out for mercy.

For most of us, however, finding our way to calmer waters is overwhelming, there are too many submersed rocks to break our hull, and good mates are hard to find. Worst of all, every sea can suddenly erupt into tsunami waves that can engulf us. Dropping anchor in rough seas is usually not an option: Once you set sail, you are obligated to find port or sink trying. Following a "short-cut" may provide some sense of euphoria, but this is at best temporary and will often lead to worse circumstances that take longer to overcome. Avoiding your Captain may also provide relief for a day or so, but he doesn't take kindly to mutiny. To be sure, once you are on your voyage, say, "Aye, aye, Captain," give God the helm, and pray day and night that you will be brought to safer waters—sooner than later.

We have all heard that wise people learn from the experiences of others. Most people I know think they are wise. Why then, do so many get hell-bent on making these experiences their own? Somehow the pursuit of happiness leads some of us into life experiences that are best avoided. Why is it that when we determine an "end" we desire, we often create "means" that are not in our best interest, much less in the best interest of others? For some reason, we think "shortcuts" will get us there more quickly when they often lead us into the deepest, most dangerous waters. Why do we put more trust in man—our friends or those we think we know—than in God, our Captain, who always leads us straight?

Those are just some questions this book will attempt to answer. I hope you will find this book will make you wiser. Life happens and stormy seas will challenge our skills and strength. Will you attempt those challenges on your own or will you give your Captain the helm? A wise boatman will determine the best headings based on the situation, take readings occasionally to confirm whether the boat is on course, and make adjustments en route to reach the destination. It is a process. Depending on the wind and seas, it may take more time or less. The open sea is a great place to improve navigation skills, but I wouldn't attempt it without our Captain.

Seek Godly wisdom—seek it diligently. Great teachers are not self-taught. They are usually well-read, have numerous experiences and stories to share, and provide you with books as suggested reading. Along the way they gained wisdom—the ability to apply knowledge and experience.

Wisdom is the principal thing; therefore get wisdom. And in all your getting, get understanding. Exalt her, and she will promote you; she will bring you honor, when you embrace her. She will place on your head an ornament of grace; a crown of glory she will deliver to you.

Proverbs 4:7–9

Through wisdom a house is built, and by understanding it is established; by knowledge the rooms are filled with all precious and pleasant riches.

Proverbs 24:3–4

No, I am not a sailor, I have never been in the Navy, and this book doesn't have all the answers. Numerous men and women have preceded me with their wisdom and I have shared some of their words and works with you. I encourage you to read their books too (you'll find a list of those I've found inspiring at the back of the book). I hope you find this book helpful as well— and I wish you smooth sailing as you embark on this spiritual journey to learn how to give God, our true Captain, control of your life.

Prologue

The Parable of the Pontoon Boat

"Would you like a pontoon boat for free?" he asked me.

When I worked with a leasing company several years ago, a broker offered me a twenty-two-foot pontoon boat for free! All I had to do was pick it up. Naturally, I asked a few questions. How old was it? Was it seaworthy? Really? Free? The broker assured me that despite its age, it was seaworthy.

He admitted, "It might need a little paint, and it would at least make a nice swimming platform. Of course, for free, there's no motor."

"Okay. I will rent a trailer and pick it up," I answered.

The boat was stored at the broker's Wisconsin lake home east of Forest Lake, Minnesota. From my home in Minneapolis, I picked up the broker in my new Pontiac Grand Am and drove to Forest Lake to rent a trailer from a boat dealer at a marina there. My cost included a long-distance phone call to Forest Lake to ensure a trailer rental and only $25 for the rental itself. "Not bad," I thought.

We got to his cabin and there the old pontoon boat rested on several cut logs. This pontoon boat was made of thick steel.

It had heavy-gauge welded steel-mesh panels on all four sides to keep riders safely onboard. These mesh panels were firmly bolted, welded, and rusted to a steel platform that was securely welded to two long steel pontoon floats. I had seen less steel when I was sightseeing at Alcatraz, I thought to myself.

You know that feeling you get when you do not want to tell someone what you really feel? I had that feeling. I wondered, "What did I get myself into?"

This broker had brought me business deals before and I was faced with a decisive moment. Should I say "no" right away and potentially eliminate a source of deals, or should I go ahead and hope this monstrosity could be fixed and serve as a swim platform?

Not sure whether I was being foolish or just being nice, I carefully backed up the Grand Am inch by inch until the trailer was under the pontoon to transfer the boat from the logs to the trailer. Something that big and old probably had a right to stay put, but I was not using all my senses at that time. We struggled tremendously to get the boat on the trailer. I began thinking I should have made the broker buy my lunch.

That's right—I had spent another $10 on lunch. I envisioned cash flying out of my wallet as I figured out what it might cost to get this behemoth in the water as a swim platform. Oh well, if nothing else, I could junk it.

A Long Ride for Reconsidering

From east of Forest Lake to my family's cabin in Bemidji, Minnesota, is no short drive. The Grand Am was struggling something fierce. Did I mention it was windy too? Once at my cabin, this monster had to come off the rental trailer. It needed much work before it could hit the water, so we inched it off onto some logs I had in the yard. This was my problem now. What an eyesore! It had taken so long to trailer it to Bemidji that we had to immediately turn around and return the trailer to the boat dealer in Forest Lake. That, too, was a long ride. The broker rode with me to and from the cabin. Thank goodness we had business deals to discuss, because I wasn't comfortable sharing my thoughts about the boat. Mostly I was quiet.

I was quietly upset and angry with myself for accepting this "free" pontoon boat. I was very quiet while I thought about what I was going to do with what seemed like several tons of steel in my yard. I think the boat sat taller than the cabin—it was certainly heavier. Yikes, what would my wife Kristin think when she saw this occupying our land? Maybe she wouldn't notice.

On the long ride back to Forest Lake to return the trailer to the rental agent and the broker to his cabin, my Grand Am didn't sound or drive right. A couple of days later I took it to the car dealer. Go figure, the transmission was shot and had to be replaced! Thank God it was under warranty. Since it was late fall and Kristin wouldn't be at the cabin until the following spring, I didn't tell her too much about the boat, except that it might make a better swim platform than a boat and that it needed a little fixing up. She gave me an "uh-uh" look and asked, "Really, a little fixing up?"

Anything—for a Price

As spring approached, I became eager to do something with the barge. I began thinking how great it was going to be. On my next visit to the cabin, I was going to fix it up. If I worked hard, this project shouldn't take too long.

When Kristin and I returned to the cabin, I realized fixing it would be a waste of time. The floats were nearly rusted through on the bottom. How could I have missed seeing that? I started checking around to see whether floats could be replaced. It didn't take me long to learn that anything can be done—for a price. Given the cost, as well as the look on Kristin's face, I decided to trash this old pontoon boat. Naturally, this proved to be easier said than done. This boat had been around for a long time— maybe it was even used to float Washington's troops across the Potomac. Why did I think I could get rid of it quickly?

Several calls later, I learned the junkyards would take it—for a fee. Instead I thought I could drag it out onto the ice in January, drill holes in the floats, wait for it to sink once the lake thawed in June, and charge scuba divers to come and see the wreck at forty feet deep. Well, it was just a thought. I was struggling now. How would I get rid of this? "Aha," I thought, "I'll cut it up into little itty-bitty pontoon pieces and sink the pieces!" Was that a smart idea or what?!

Let's see, with a reciprocating saw ($200+) and no less than twenty heavy-duty carbide bi-metal blades later (short and long blades at $2 to $3 each), plus what seemed like three or four years of hard labor, I was making some headway. Ferrous metals or not, sparks were flying, my right arm jerked my head and neck about, and the triple-plated rails, fencing, angle-irons, and platform were cut down to three- by four-foot pieces. Gosh, those blades lost their teeth quickly and bent something fierce when they hit metal and kicked back!

All I had to do was to drag these floats onto the water, pull them out to the deep area of the lake, drill some larger holes in them, and sink those rusty things! Not so fast. They were filled with foam. (Did they use foam back in 1776? I was surprised I hadn't found tea bags in there!) Testing the seals and connections between the floats' foam and steel skin as well as assessing the thickness of steel and welded joints proved that battleship technology in 1776 was excellent. Except for the lack of rustproof paint, they really did make things stronger back then.

Using a long blade, I made a cut into the float. Like the other steel parts, this too was about one-eighth inch or thicker. I cut the float in half and then into smaller sections…well, I tried. Even then, the blown-in foam wasn't going to come out, not even when I used a crowbar. So I cut each section lengthwise, which didn't work either. I couldn't separate the foam from the filleted steel! What was holding these together? At last, I found a couple of internal plates, cut around them to quarter the entire float, and then quartered two of the four sections to release the foam's grip. The pointed ends would have to go to the dump. I had no idea what that would cost me—I had lost track of the total cost by this point.

Mind you, I still had one more float to cut. At least by then I knew what I was up against. Nearing the end of my strength, I switched gears and started hauling the scraps to my 1950s Lund fishing boat with its ancient motor. Inside the fishing boat, I could haul about four sheets of steel and smaller cuts at one time. I found a perfect thirty-five-foot-deep area of the lake that I thought could use more structure to shelter fish, and I threw out a marker. I circled around, anchored, and began heaving the steel pieces toward the marker. Ouch, the rusty metal scratched my arms. Oh, well, a mere flesh wound. No problem, I had had a tetanus shot recently. Nothing was going to stop me now!

Beginning to Sink

Back I went to the dock to get another load. I was ready to make the next trip when Kristin asked to join me. Perhaps it looked like I was having fun. What man doesn't enjoy throwing large ragged steel chunks overboard toward a target? Are you kidding? I was finally accomplishing something. Caked in sweat and grime, I was grinning from ear to ear with steel shavings between my teeth and cuts across my hands and arms! What else could possibly happen?

While we took this load out onto the lake, though, there seemed to be a little more water around our feet, but I made no mention of this. Kristin did, however. "Mark, there is water coming into the boat!" she said.

I blew off her comment as though I knew what I was talking about. "Don't worry about it, honey. All old boats take on a little water." I said. I picked up the last ragged steel sheet and heaved it overboard. I was finally done! The old pontoon boat was no longer in our yard. It was time to rejoice!

Except that there was a little fountain of water spurting up from the bottom of the Lund. I had a hole in my boat! "Kristin, start bailing water while I get us back to the dock!" I ordered. I was captain of the boat, you know. Well, at least I thought I was.

Kristin and I made it back. With her bailing water and my quick reaction to head back to shore, we survived with only wet feet. We pulled the boat onto the shore and I stared at the hole in my fishing boat. By now I was thinking the free pontoon boat I had hauled, dismantled, and sunk had become more expensive than a new twenty-four-foot aluminum pontoon boat with a 50-horsepower motor, bimini top, and a load of extras.

Why didn't I just say "No, thanks," when I first saw the rusty pontoon boat? On second thought, that broker didn't really help me with deals that much. Why had I been sooooo stupid? One boat sunk—and another boat that almost sank and now needed repair. At this point I could not even afford to think about how "free" that pontoon was.

Thank goodness Kristin's father kindly brought another fishing boat to the cabin for use that summer—at least I could still fish!

Chapter 1

Attracted by the Lure

> *Now the serpent was more cunning than any beast of the field which the LORD God had made. And he said to the woman, "Has God indeed said, 'You shall not eat of every tree of the garden'?"*
>
> Genesis 3:1

> *Then the devil, taking Him up on a high mountain, showed Him all the kingdoms of the world in a moment of time. And the devil said to Him, "All this authority I will give You, and their glory; for this has been delivered to me, and I give it to whomever I wish."*
>
> Luke 4:5–6

"Would you like a pontoon boat for free?" he asked me....All I had to do was pick it up. Naturally, I asked a few questions. How old was it? Was it seaworthy? Really? Free? The broker assured me that despite its age, it was

seaworthy....He admitted, "It might need a little paint, and it would at least make a nice swimming platform. Of course, for free, there's no motor." (from "The Parable of the Pontoon Boat")

Beware of conversing with the "enemy." The enemy will give you thoughts that enter your head. The enemy may lure you where you didn't intend to go.

A lure is an enticement that suggests some advantage or pleasure to be gained. It is similar to being tempted. The lure is the fruit of the tree of knowledge or gaining all the kingdoms of the world. A lure is provocative. For me, that pontoon boat was a provocative lure that proved to offer a relatively small lesson. The pontoon boat as a metaphor is meant to give you a somewhat comical picture and a demonstration of life's lessons that are not all that comical when they happen but provide fodder for laughter at a later time. Sometimes it takes a long time to be able to look back and laugh. Well, it seems as though it takes only one or two seconds for my wife Kristin to look at my situations and laugh at me. Of course, she claims she is laughing *with* me.

A lure, if you are not careful, will likely be an opportunity for a lesson. Lessons are known by many names: *trials, tests, tribulations,* and *experiences,* among other terms. The Lord was kind enough to provide me with many lessons throughout my youth—usually with my brother Paul. For example, when I was in sixth grade and Paul in fifth, I had a kid's chemistry set that I kept on a desk in our screen porch. One night while a babysitter was caring for us,

I was busy with my chemistry set. Paul saw the Bunsen burner and suggested that if we put a paper bag over the lit burner, the bag would rise from the hot air. I told Paul that it would be dangerous and that the bag could catch on fire, but somehow he convinced me it would rise and not burn. Well, you can imagine what happened: The thin paper lunch bag burst into flames. Paul blew on the fire and the flaming bag fell to the floor. I quickly stomped out the fire, but the damage was done. The carpet was burned. I moved the desk to cover the burn and hoped my parents wouldn't see it when they returned. Fat chance. The sitter ratted on us and we were disciplined immediately.

These episodes were opportunities for me to listen and learn. You might think such life experiences would have given me a better foundation for discernment. Admittedly, I must have had a very stubborn heart and a hard head, because the Lord determined that I needed more trials and test into my adult years. Some of these more recent experiences still carry wounds with fresh scars. Kristin and I are just beginning to look back and smile, for example, about one recent experience involving a real estate deal, which I'll share with you later. We are *smiling*, not looking back in any sort of "I won" proud or gloating way with laughter. Instead we are looking back and *glad* that we learned, forgave, and moved on (or at least are moving on). I reminded myself, we shouldn't rejoice when our enemy falls (see Proverbs 24:17–18).

And whenever you stand praying, if you have anything against anyone, forgive him, that your Father in heaven may also forgive you your trespasses. But if you do not forgive, neither will your Father in heaven forgive your trespasses.

Mark 11:25–26

Big Battles and Huge Oceans

Often we feel as though we are sitting in a sixteen-foot rowboat on the ocean and are utterly helpless.

The Bible says much about the topic of forgiveness. John Bevere's book *The Bait of Satan, Your Response Determines Your Future* provides excellent examples of how your reaction to offenses can be deadly traps. It is best to realize that forgiveness is needed no matter the type of lesson we're learning. Forgiveness is an act of my will. I do all I can to forgive in the way God does, entirely, without keeping a record of wrongs. Whether I feel it or not is irrelevant.

There are small battles and Big Battles! There are lakes and then there are Huge Oceans! Often we feel as though we are sitting in a sixteen-foot rowboat on the ocean and are utterly helpless. We have called on the Lord and begged for mercy, pleaded the Blood of Christ, prayed for at least two minutes at a stretch, stepped it up a notch by praying in tongues, cried tears until no more fell from our flushed cheeks, wrestled throughout a sleepless night, and all to no avail. Doesn't it seem as though we are isolated from help and forgotten by our Heavenly Father, left to die in raging waters?

We are in agony. Have you ever felt alone when fighting your Biggest Battles? Our faith begins to dwindle, doubt creeps into our thoughts and speech, and self-condemnation begins to dominate our thoughts. We probably did do something wrong, repented, asked for forgiveness, and thought we were forgiven. Shortly afterward, though, our circumstances did not go away and the battle looked bigger and the waves looked higher than ever.

Worse, our weapons seemed small and useless. The feeling of being forgiven has faded. Fear, shame, and doubt have gained strength. In a moment we felt strong and victorious in the strength of the Lord. Just as quickly it changed to the agony of defeat. One moment I am lifting up my spouse with encouragement. A day later she is lifting me up with encouragement. There have been times when we both shared feelings of victory and encouragement together only to face what seemed like a setback in the next hour or day. At times, it did not take much to steal our hope and challenge our faith.

Caught in such a Big Battle, I pressed inward. I started a daily journal. Best of all, I fasted from using the snooze button on my alarm clock and made sure I gave myself time to get into God's Word before I left for work. I journaled my study of God's Word, dreams given to me by the Holy Spirit, affirmations I created or borrowed from godly sources, and more. Listening to my pastors, Timothy and Cherrié Peterson, I immersed myself in victory and prosperity verses from the Bible, listened to numerous godly messages, and read related books.

Noah and the Wildernesses

Pastor Timothy Peterson gave me an opportunity to teach about Noah's experience in the ark one Wednesday class night. I had shared my outline with a friend at church. God speaks in many ways, for through that friend, who served as a messenger from God at that moment, I was given a message on a CD taught by Matt Sorger of Matt Sorger Ministries. Sorger discussed five wildernesses: the wildernesses of transition, testing, consecration, intimacy, and rebellion. I had always thought there was just one wilderness and it didn't seem to be a great place for the Jews. If they had not rebelled, maybe their time in that wilderness would have been eleven days and not forty years (see Deuteronomy 1:2–3). Maybe they all would have entered the Promised Land and into the Glory of God!

As I began to think more about Noah, I realized he was found righteous in the Lord's sight but would have also been a sinner like you and me. That is, we all fall short of the glory of God. Noah wasn't perfect, but he was not being punished either. He was, however, in a sense captive in the ark! The truth is that he was being protected. Further, I must be the dense one (I guess I established that earlier), but I thought it rained for forty days and nights. Not so fast. Noah and his family were in the ark for one year and ten days! Looking closer, while Noah and his family were in the ark being tossed about for several months with all those smelly animals, my Bible says in Genesis 8:1, *"Then God remembered Noah..."* What?! Only one family exists on all the earth, and the Lord *then* remembered Noah was stuck in the ark! Was the Lord taking a nap, floating on a raft somewhere contemplating the Great Tribulation, or determining when he would release Christ Jesus to earth to give us all redemption should we choose His way?

Just like that, my perspective changed! The Lord uses one or more wildernesses to prepare us for new levels of maturity, wisdom, and authority! For Noah and his family, it was a new beginning and household salvation. Similar to John the Baptist, Noah was set apart from the world to be consecrated and prepared for a new beginning! Like John the Baptist, Noah and his family were in the wilderness of consecration.

The Jews were in a wilderness of transition from slavery to life in the Promised Land when they entered a wilderness of rebellion characterized by backsliding, complaining, and doubting God. Don't go there—the Jews extended their stay more than thirty-nine years. We learn that Jesus was led to the wilderness by the Holy Spirit to be tested and tried, and using the Word as His weapon, He came out with power and authority. We can also be lured into the Valley of Achor ("Achor" meaning valley of "trouble") and from there we are given our vineyards and a door of hope (see Hosea 2:14-15). In this valley, we walk with the Lord. This wilderness is a place of intimacy with the Lord, where the Lord says "...you will call Me 'My Husband'" (verse 16). We want to dwell in this wilderness at all times.

No matter how difficult the circumstances, the experience will prepare you for something greater if you determine to learn and accept the lessons from God, your Captain.

Are you wandering in a wilderness wondering where or when you can find your way? Each wilderness is a place to prepare us for something greater. When you fully grasp that you are a child of God, a chosen one, and one He wishes to teach so you can promote the Gospel with power and authority, you too will begin to appreciate the circumstances that seem to overwhelm you at times. No matter how difficult the circumstances, the experience will prepare you for something greater if you determine to learn and accept the lessons from God, your Captain.

Door of Hope by Mark Kuhne

Testing and trials do not end. Luke tells us that the devil will return. In fact, he may return when it is in his best interest, not yours. On the other hand, with a different perspective, when he returns may be your very best time. It may be at a time when you are ready to grow and are better equipped to handle bigger and rougher seas in your journey with Christ. Maybe you are being emptied so you can be filled!

> *Now when the devil had ended every temptation, he departed from Him until an opportune time.*
>
> Luke 4:13

Lessons in Covetousness

If you are a parent, for example, you can relate to lessons you teach your children, and you wish they would learn those lessons sooner than later! Taking away the circumstances too soon or indulging your child doesn't have the same impact and often negates the entire lesson. No doubt, the child will usually be lured again, return to the same circumstances, and face the test again. Seeing your child learn from the lesson, however, gives you immense satisfaction. The child will likely handle those circumstances differently in the future. The child's perspective will have changed.

It is no different for our Heavenly Father to see us learn from testing and trials. Invite the Holy Spirit to show you in tangible ways what you need to know and learn so you can journey into new territory. If you dare, ask the Lord to refine you by fire so you can be a mighty force in His kingdom!

What is the Lord removing when refining us in fire? In Zechariah 13:9, God says *"I...will refine them as silver is refined...,"* and in Daniel 11:35, *"And some of those...shall fall, to refine them, purify them...,"* and in Isaiah 1:25, *"And thoroughly purge away your dross...."* Why is fire needed? Fire liquefies the metal, allowing dross to rise to the surface. Dross is scum—impurities—that forms on the surface of molten metal. As long as we remain "hard," that is, stubborn to righteous or godly thinking or irreverent, our impurities cannot be removed and calamity follows.

> *Happy is the man who is always reverent, But he who hardens his heart will fall into calamity."*
>
> Proverbs 28:14

Impurities include the desires of our heart when they are not aligned with the Lord's desires. God wants us to seek His heart and to do His will, as conveyed in Acts 13:22: *"...He raised up for them David as king, to whom also He gave testimony and said, 'I have found David the son of Jesse, a man after My own heart, who will do all My will.'"* In James 1:14–15, with respect to the desires of the flesh, we are tempted when we are *"drawn away by"* our *"own desires,"* not the Lord's desire. Mark says out of our heart proceeds covetousness (see Mark 7:21-22). What is *covetousness* really? The Webster dictionary describes *covetousness* as a "strong or inordinate desire of obtaining and possessing some supposed good." It is a desire or wish for something with eagerness. Covetousness is an earnest desire. It can be good when we covet after the Lord's will for us (*"...earnestly desire the best gifts...,"* 1 Corinthians 12:31), or bad (*"...you shall not covet your neighbor's wife...,"* Exodus 20:17). Generally, it is more often associated with a wrongful lust to possess something.

> *And He said to them, "Take heed and beware of covetousness, for one's life does not consist in the abundance of things he possesses."*
>
> Luke 12:15

> *Let your conduct be without covetousness; be content with such things as you have.*
>
> Hebrews 13:5

It is the *lust* for material riches that leads to greediness. Money in itself is not evil. If you are content with what the Lord has already given you, you will be less apt to fall prey to the lure of excess desires. Long after the pontoon boat fiasco, a big lesson from that familiar coveting spirit—at least familiar now as I look back—was looming on my horizon! The parable of the pontoon boat closely parallels another real-life story of mine, but relatively speaking, the pontoon boat dilemma was a small problem. Huge waves were headed my way! Was I prepared? My main reason for writing this book—a Big Battle involving finances—provided much *bigger* waves to overcome.

> I choose to act or not act. Decisions are my responsibility to discern.

Have you ever noticed that certain people or personality types are able to penetrate your filters of discernment and lure you into what should have remained their opportunities or problems? Why? What is it about them that helps make what they offer so attractive? As I mentioned earlier, my brother Paul was one of those people in my life who could sometimes talk me into a paper bag of snakes—even when I knew there were snakes in the bag! Now I admit that suggesting others do things to you is looking at life with a victim mentality. It is rare that others make you do anything. I choose to act or not act. Decisions are my responsibility to discern. My own choices led me into a Big Battle involving a real estate investment.

Bear in mind that my perception of what is a Big Battle is not necessary your perception of what is a Big Battle. You may have something far bigger or much smaller. It doesn't really matter. What matters is that we perceive certain circumstances to be worse than others. What matters is that we seek victory over or through our circumstances. Admittedly, my circumstances had the potential to be big mostly because of the emphasis or weight I placed on them. In fact, it was my "perception" that changed everything; during the course of the battle, the circumstances hardly changed at all. So what happened?

Before the Big Waves, a Housing Bubble

A person I knew and trusted for many years was a realtor in Nevada. He was successfully investing in preconstruction real estate opportunities in the range of $150,000 to $250,000. By 2004, he had already bought a few and sold them prior to completion for a profit. He wasn't alone in this endeavor. Many people in numerous states were investing and selling preconstruction properties. He came across opportunities that were $500,000 or more. By early 2005, he had brought them to my attention and wondered whether I knew people who might have an interest.

Given the cost of these planned housing units, the 10 percent to 20 percent required deposits were substantial. This was just the deposit. Upon completion of construction and shortly after a certificate of occupancy was issued, you were suppose to buy the unit and pay the balance, for example.

As an alternative, an investor could sell the unit on or before the closing. The idea is that the market would drive up the unit's value during the construction period so (1) you make a profit on your investment and (2) you wouldn't need to pay the balance at closing, because the new homeowners (or their bank through their new mortgage) would. Your profit would be the house's increase in value during construction, minus your deposit. In other words, you transfer the opportunity to someone else: They essentially pay back your deposit plus a little more for you originating the opportunity. You net a little profit. This investing worked well for quite a while—as long as there was continued demand for housing, traditional mortgage lending practices occurred, and housing developments' values rose during construction.

Especially between 2006 and 2009, however, millions of investors and homeowners lost value in their real estate positions. As I recall, it had been predicted before 2005 that there was a "housing bubble," but most people did not believe it. The housing bubble involved too much housing inventory available and not enough qualified buyers. Some experts also said housing values were overpriced and too many homeowners held mortgages they couldn't afford. Many of these mortgages had adjustable interest rates, which eventually led to burdensome payment requirements.

When the housing bubble burst, home foreclosures skyrocketed and thousands of houses, townhomes, and condominiums flooded the market, raising inventory to all-time high levels. Based on the age-old "supply and demand" theory—I think coined before the time of Moses—with inventory of housing extremely high, prices dropped. With housing values down, those who had invested deposits on preconstruction real estate projects were unable or unwilling to close on their units. In most cases, investors walked away from their deposits: They didn't close on their purchase agreement contracts and they forfeited their deposits. Even if you didn't invest in speculation real estate, many of you were also

41

likely affected by the bubble bursting; many of you have felt the pain in knowing that your home value has dropped.

Before the housing bubble burst, the Nevada realtor came to me looking for potential leads, and I gave him a few names to pursue. A few decided to invest. Some shared information about these real estate investments with others. More than one person asked me as a banker to help them finance their deposits. These investors had high net-worth positions. Some used their home equity as collateral to secure loans. A few obtained unsecured loans. As the market deteriorated, many of these investors became delinquent and their loans went unpaid. As a result, lending guidelines today are much tighter than they were then.

A Lure in Nevada

One investor in particular—I'll call him Jesse, a client of mine since 2003—was about to go to Nevada to look into these pre-construction housing development investments. Based on the amount of loans he had outstanding at the bank, he was a fairly significant client. He asked me to meet him in Las Vegas. It was winter. Flights to Las Vegas were cheap. I had known and respected Jesse for about two years. Why not?

I flew to Nevada and joined Jesse for a few hours to see various properties. After all, as a lender it would be good for me to see these types of investment properties with my own eyes. After seeing a few properties, we met to eat before I headed back home. During the conversation Jesse surprised me by saying,

"I would like to bless you and share this opportunity with you."
Jesse was planning to make a deposit on an expensive townhome
not far from Las Vegas. Whether Jesse had strong religious beliefs
and actually believed it would be a blessing to me or whether
Jesse had caught onto my beliefs and was intentionally using the
word *bless* to influence me, I don't know.

"I would like to bless you and share this opportunity with you,"
he said.

I replied, "I couldn't. I do not have that kind of money. This is
way out of my league!"

As I recall, Jesse said, "You don't need any money; you'll be
blessed after they are sold."

I was surprised, flustered, and flattered. I also had no reason to
believe that Jesse, a wealthy person, was going to share his capital gain with me out of the kindness of his heart. Maybe it was
one of his investment strategies to share the risk. Co-investing is
common at investments with high levels of risk, but technically
he wasn't asking me to co-invest. Maybe he felt better about
himself when offering opportunities to others. Maybe it was
exciting for him to make such offers. I do not know.

As I said, I immediately made it clear that this investment was out
of my league. But out of politeness and without giving it much
thought, my second reaction was "Why not?" It would be a long
time before these units would be finished. Anything could happen.

Maybe this would be one of those "once in a lifetime" events that would change my life. But I thought chances were that Jesse would forget about our conversation. I had absolutely nothing to put into his investment. I had no idea how he would include me at a later date. How does that saying go? Time would tell.

Warned of Wild Animals

If you are in the jungle and you hear a lion, be vigilant, watchful, circumspect, attentive to avoid danger—and have the good sense to avoid the beast!

God warns us in many ways. How does God usually speak to you? He often speaks to me through dreams and visions. In 2004, I had a dream involving two people I knew. Bruce, a client of mine, and Rick a friend of his whom I also knew, were casually walking together. They were fifty to a hundred yards from me and walking away. I was left behind with a lion. The lion was looking for me, hunting me down. I was hiding as best I could from the lion. The lion didn't get me, but I wondered why the lion didn't go after them. Why was the lion only after me? They were in the open and easy for the lion to pursue. I was hidden. I didn't understand.

Sometime later I was walking with this client. I recalled this dream about the lion and shared it with him. He said that Rick and he had the protection of the Lord and that I needed to stand up to the lion, who was Satan, and to realize that God would protect me. Considering that I thought these two men were stronger in the Lord than I was at the time, his explanation made sense. Knowing that the lion represented Satan and knowing I could resist the devil by standing up to him made me feel stronger. And I never had that dream again. Case closed! (Or so it seemed....)

Be careful whom you listen to when asking for your dreams and visions to be interpreted, for the devil can take the truth and twist it. In hindsight, I learned later that Bruce lured Rick astray in a bogus financial investment. In my dream they had walked away together: It had made sense to me then that those two were the protected ones. Later, I realized that the lion in the dream was no longer interested in what he already had devoured. The lion was after me to destroy me too.

Unfortunately, I didn't take the time to understand God's warning then. Unfortunately, I didn't seek another opinion. Unfortunately, my misunderstandings led me to misplaced trust in a man and to entering into a snare that became a huge battle in my life. Satan roars like a lion. If you are in the jungle and you hear a lion, be vigilant, watchful, circumspect, attentive to avoid danger—and have the good sense to avoid the beast!

"Be sober, be vigilant; because your adversary the devil walks about like a roaring lion, seeking whom he may devour."

1 Peter 5:8

45

Oddly enough, earlier that year, I had had another dream that also had warned me. (Was I dense or what?) In that dream, a grizzly bear was near me, feeding or looking for food. I was not hunting but I stood in a hunting tree stand. The stand was several feet off the ground, but not so high that this grizzly bear couldn't stand and be within claws' reach of my feet. The bear was foraging under the tree stand. I was understandably concerned and afraid. Grizzly bears are huge and unpredictable. This hunting tree stand was more like a cage, though. I was sitting in this cage-like structure strapped to this tree, but my feet were vulnerable to attack. I felt vulnerable, but somewhat protected. I did not have an ear to hear the Lord, but He was trying to tell me to be careful.

"He has been to me a bear lying in wait, like a lion in ambush."

Lamentations 3:10

Months after my dreams, a simple conversation with Jesse provided a lure that eventually led into a trap. It was a trap I could have easily avoided if I had been paying attention. If I had an ear to hear and an eye to see—if only I had given the helm to God sooner!

Chapter 2

Taking the Bait

> *So when the woman saw that the tree was good for food, that it was pleasant to the eyes, and a tree desirable to make one wise, she took of its fruit and ate. She also gave to her husband with her, and he ate.*
>
> Genesis 3:6

"Okay. I will rent a trailer and pick it up," I answered....I picked up the broker and drove to rent a trailer from a boat dealer at a marina there. My cost included a long-distance phone call to ensure a trailer rental and only $25 for the rental itself. "Not bad," I thought. (from "The Parable of the Pontoon Boat")

Do not hold or take possession of the bait intended to lure you. Consuming it quickly follows. Michael Cameneti, author of *The Missing Ingredient to Success*, writes, "The key is to be convicted and constrained not to yield to the temptation before you ever act on it."

How do you know what is bait? It may be obvious and clearly forbidden, as was the fruit in the Garden of Eden. Not all bait is so obvious: alcohol, prescription drugs, cigarettes, gambling,

47

and more come to mind. Bait is an "allurement, enticement, temptation to draw or lure you to a hook or snare. Once you are hooked, it is hard to get free.

Some not-so-obvious hooks pull you in slowly, little by little. The Christian rock band Casting Crowns sings a great song that describes this as a "slow fade":

Slow Fade

Be careful little eyes what you see
It's the second glance that ties your hands as darkness pulls the strings
Be careful little feet where you go
For it's the little feet behind you that are sure to follow

It's a slow fade when you give yourself away
It's a slow fade when black and white have turned to gray
Thoughts invade, choices are made, a price will be paid
When you give yourself away
People never crumble in a day
It's a slow fade, it's a slow fade

Be careful little ears what you hear
When flattery leads to compromise, the end is always near
Be careful little lips what you say
For empty words and promises lead broken hearts astray

It's a slow fade when you give yourself away
It's a slow fade when black and white have turned to gray

Taking the Bait

Thoughts invade, choices are made, a price will be paid
When you give yourself away
People never crumble in a day
The journey from your mind to your hands
Is shorter than you're thinking
Be careful if you think you stand
You just might be sinking

It's a slow fade when you give yourself away
It's a slow fade when black and white have turned to gray
Thoughts invade, choices are made, a price will be paid
When you give yourself away
People never crumble in a day
Daddies never crumble in a day
Families never crumble in a day

Oh be careful little eyes what see
Oh be careful little eyes what you see
For the Father up above is looking down in love
Oh be careful little eyes what you see

As far as the pontoon boat was concerned, I didn't see the trailer rental, even loading the boat on the trailer, as the beginning of a slow fade. The idea of taking the boat still sounded good and I did not envision any trouble. The uphill battle to get it on the trailer did not feel like going down a slippery slope.

Holding onto the bait in and of itself doesn't *always* make you take it, but it certainly puts you much closer to taking it. The impetus toward taking the bait becomes very strong at that point. Stopping before taking a "bite" is much more difficult once that lure, that bait, is in your hands. The bait, whatever it is, looks wonderful. The colors are to die for. It feels terrific as you roll your hands over it. This is going to be great. Just imagine how it is going to taste when you eat this fruit.

Some Bait You Can't Hold

Let's consider another possible example, one without a tangible thing as the bait. Maybe a friend or acquaintance says, "I have this business proposition and I would like you to join me. Everyone who is doing this is making more money than they ever dreamed about." You reply, "But I don't know anything about that type of business."

Your friend reassures, "That's okay; I am an expert on this!"

You say, "I don't have the capital to invest in this. I don't earn that kind of money. I have never had that much money in savings."

"That's okay," says your friend.

"Let me think about it and talk to my wife," you say. You practically skip away. Someone likes you enough to want to help you get ahead financially! This may be your big break in life. You have waited a long time for a breakthrough. This could be it!

You spend the rest of day imagining how great life could be after you too make all that money. Imagine how you could use the funds to promote the Gospel. Yes, you begin to make it sound really good and godly. This isn't about the love of money; it is about the great things you could do with that amount of money. It is about building the Kingdom of God! You have no intention of using the money you make to only serve yourself and your family. No, you imagine great plans that appear righteous. No one could possibly blame you for using money to serve others.

Happy as can be, you arrive home and begin to tell your wife all about this great opportunity! She sees your excitement. She hasn't seen you this happy for a long time. "Honey, you have got to hear this!" you tell her, explaining that so-and-so has a great business opportunity and wants to include the two of you.

She wonders, "Why would that person want to do that for you, for us?"

"Because he wants to be nice to me," you reassure her. "This is our big break. Finally, we are getting ahead, things are great at work, and this is one more way for God to bless us!"

You get the picture—and probably see the parallel I'm drawing to my experience with Jesse. In that situation, Jesse was so successful himself that I figured he knew what he was doing. He and his family lived in a huge house, drove expensive cars, had a cabin-cruiser on a nearby river, traveled to great destinations where they rented an entire house with maids and cooks, and seemed to be big givers at charitable events.

No paperwork, no deal. Remember that! No paperwork, no deal. Before you sign any paperwork, have it reviewed by another skilled set of eyes. Seek advice.

As I looked around in the marketplace, I saw many entrepreneurs and real estate investors doing very well. The person who had approached me had been making money in real estate investments for years. I trusted him. I figured it could not possibly hurt for me to go along—after all, it wouldn't even cost me anything!

In anticipation of this future blessing—whatever that would be—I went online and created a limited liability company, or LLC, for Jesse and me. In short, it was a company, but not a sole proprietorship (individual) or partnership-type organization. The LLC wasn't capitalized, meaning it wasn't funded, was just a "shell."

Creating the LLC was cheap and, I thought, could easily be discontinued. So to my credit, I was thinking through a few "what ifs," although I was not seeing the whole picture. How could I get hurt? I don't recall really asking, "How can this go wrong?" Did I define the upside as well as the downside? "What downside?" I should have asked. "Just in case it doesn't work out, who is going to pay for what? What do you mean, pay for what? Do you have paperwork to describe the obligations, if any?"

In other words, I was fixated on the proverbial wave and not seeing the ocean. I wasn't looking for the downside, the undertow. I certainly didn't consider choppy seas or worse! Maybe in the same situation you would be wise enough to have been thinking of the downside, but I wasn't—at least not at first.

Before creating a legal entity, such as a LLC, is the perfect time to describe who is going to do what, how, when, where, and why as it relates to income as well as, heaven forbid, a loss. No paperwork, no deal. Remember that! No paperwork, no deal. Before you sign any paperwork, have it reviewed by another skilled set of eyes. Seek advice.

Familiarity Breeds Trust—and Gullibility

Why is it that certain personalities seem to be able to draw us in where we should not go? Before you assume I mean the snake, consider this: Eve's husband was *with* her. He also knew better than to eat the fruit of that particular tree. Whether Adam took the time to examine the fruit himself didn't matter. Both Adam and Eve got into trouble. After God found them hiding their *nakedness,* Adam blamed Eve and said, *"...The woman whom You gave to be with me, she gave me of the tree, and I ate"* (Genesis 3:12). Eve blamed the serpent and said, *"...The serpent deceived me, and I ate"* (verse 13). Both Adam and Eve were guilty. Both felt shame. Both were punished.

We are no different. Sometimes we take the bait just because we are with people we know. We make assumptions that they already did the research, the homework, the "due diligence." Maybe we believe that they are the experts so we rely on their judgment. Claiming ignorance and blaming someone else will rarely get you out of your trouble, though, at least not with God.

Steven M.R. Covey, author of the book *The Speed of Trust*, discusses how to build trust quickly: Say what you mean and mean what you say, be prepared to be vulnerable and willing to admit your own mistakes, and underpromise and overdeliver. Covey also discusses how we become gullible. He shows that where there is high trust *and* low analysis (lack of due diligence or discernment), a person is gullible.

Whether you are completely gullible, however, also depends on whom you trust. My wife and I, for example, trust each other explicitly and rarely question each other. Does that make us gullible? Not necessarily in all ways, but in some ways, yes. In areas where we do not have much expertise, we have now learned to seek advice and put more effort into discernment and our analysis. My wife Kristin notes that in Proverbs 19:2 we are reminded *"...it is not good for a soul to be without knowledge, and he sins who hastens with his feet."*

Expert or Prey?

You become prey when you step out of your area of expertise.

You become prey when you step out of your area of expertise. Read that carefully again: You *become* prey *when* you step out of your area of expertise. You are less likely to be gullible in your area of expertise. Despite being an expert, you may make a mistake occasionally. External circumstances, sources of information, or market or economic conditions may throw you off at times, but you are most likely to face only calculated losses or small battles that are in your comfort zone. When you venture outside of your area of expertise, though, you become prey. And who looks for prey? Predators.

A prudent man foresees evil and hides himself; the simple pass on and are punished.

Proverbs 27:12

Predators plunder, pillage, and seize by violence to devour their prey. Have you ever watched a *National Geographic* television program that shows a pride of female lions taking down a zebra? Once in the grip of the lions' jaws, the zebra stands no chance of survival. The lions tear open its flesh and eat before the zebra is even dead. Have you seen video of a monster crocodile pulling a wildebeest underwater? The crocodile turns the wildebeest over and over. Limbs, tails, water, and mud are thrashed about. Then, all appears calm. The wildebeest gives up and dies. I apologize for the graphic visual imagery, but being prey in the natural world generally involves violence. Being devoured isn't pretty on the plains of Africa, and being devoured metaphorically isn't pretty when it happens to you or me.

The opposite of Proverbs 3:5-6 is trust in man with all your heart, lean not unto your own understanding. In all ways acknowledge that man, and he will direct your path. I have been there, and done that! One could say that is from the Old Counterfeit Version.

Certainly you cannot be an expert and "safe" at everything, but you do not need to step outside of your boundaries and become prey. Life does become more dangerous when you wander away from your place (see Proverbs 27:8). And, yes, there are times when we are new at something, learning and exploring unfamiliar territory—but we do not need to be on our own and venture onto the plains of Africa without a guide, without being outfitted with proper equipment for the journey.

> Know that when God gives you an assignment, He also supplies the provisions and tools.

Just remember, not only did God frame the worlds (see Hebrews 11:3), but God formed you (see Psalm 139:13, Isaiah 43:7, Isaiah 44:2). He made your parts in your mother's womb (see Psalm 139:13). He has made you to give you special assignments in certain seasons. He has given you unique gifts and talents to carry out your assignments. In other words, you are uniquely made to be a certain person to accomplish special jobs. Know that when God gives you an assignment, He also supplies the provisions and tools. Sometimes these tools may be untapped resources within ourselves, and other times they come in the form of help from others. Provisions could also be skills and abilities that can be used to generate income or gains. Or maybe you have something that can be traded, as in bartering a good or service for another good or service. The point is, you probably already have many of the provisions you need to do what you are called to do.

Staying on Assignment

From Moses in the Old Testament to Paul in the New Testament, numerous men and women were called by the Lord to their assignments. As Pastor Timothy Peterson told us in a class covering Bible characters, Moses was called by the Lord—*"Come now, therefore, and I will send you to Pharaoh that you may bring My people, the children of Israel, out of Egypt"* (Exodus 3:10)—and then he was commissioned. Between the call and the commission, a person becomes prepared for the call. As you prepare, you tap into the provisions and tools God provides, gain some expertise, and reduce your chances of being preyed upon.

Where are you with your call? Are you on track? Or did you give up during the preparation process? If you've given up, did you have plenty of excuses why you couldn't perform your call? If you did, you are in good company. The Bible shows us the human side of many characters in the Bible who had excuses. Moses, for example, had four excuses:

1. I am inadequate: *"Who am I that I should go to Pharaoh, and that I should bring the children of Israel out of Egypt?"* (Exodus 3:11)

2. What is relevant about Your name to the Pha-

raoh? In other words, this was a relationship issue in that Moses didn't know God very well yet. *Then Moses said to God, "Indeed, when I come to the children of Israel and say to them, 'The God of your fathers has sent me to you,' and they say to me, 'What is His name?' What shall I say to them?"* (Exodus 3:13)

3. They won't believe or listen to me. *Then Moses answered and said, "But suppose they will not believe me or listen to my voice; suppose they say, 'The LORD has not appeared to you.'"* (Exodus 4:1)

4. I don't speak very well. *Then Moses said to the LORD, "O my Lord, I am not eloquent, neither before nor since You have spoken to Your servant; but I am slow of speech and slow of tongue."* (Exodus 4:10)

Did you quit when tests and trials got too hard, too much to handle? Like Moses, do you question your abilities and look for a way out? Or did you quit because you didn't like the call? Again, you would be in good company. Jonah was called: *"Arise, go to Nineveh, that great city, and cry out against it; for their wickedness has come up before Me"* (Jonah 1:2). Jonah was quick, however, to turn the other direction: *"But Jonah arose to flee to Tarshish from the presence of the LORD. He went down to Joppa, and found a ship going to Tarshish; so he paid the fare, and went down into it, to go with them to Tarshish from the presence of the LORD"* (Jonah 1:3).

Jonah ran away! But God gave him a second chance—even if it did involve being swallowed by a giant fish. Isn't God great? Even when we think we are running away, He uses those circumstances to prepare us for our call and the commission. How many of us want to be thrown into the sea to find ourselves in the belly of a large fish? How many of you feel you are there right now? If you are tired of your three-day, three-night diversion, maybe it is time to do what you were called to do.

> *But indeed, O man, who are you to reply against God? Will the thing formed say to Him who formed it, "Why have you made me like this?" Does not the potter have the power over the clay…?*
>
> Romans 9:20–21

One test to figure out whether you should be doing something differently is to take inventory of your provisions. What is in your hand or in your possession? If you do not have the provisions, that is not to say that God will not provide you with what you need along the way, but lack of provisions alone would be a reason for caution, to step out carefully and slowly, one step at a time. If there is any indication that in going forward the cost exceeds what you can afford to lose, pull back. One's cost may be emotional as well as financial. To build a ship that can handle the ocean will likely require millions of dollars and access to a port. On the other hand, to build a canoe, the cash requirements and tools will be considerably different, less costly. You should know that the Lord your God will not forsake you.

God doesn't want you to lose so much that you go into utter financial (or emotional) failure. Investments or opportunities need to be explored and examined before you commit yourself beyond what you can afford to lose. That desire you have to move in that investment or opportunity needs to be examined objectively. What knowledge do you have or have access to? Who else do you know and trust who can provide you another set of eyes? If you are unsure about asking others about an opportunity, that too should cause you to step back cautiously and open your eyes wider. Remember that Proverbs 19:2—*"Also it is not good for a soul to be without knowledge, and he sins who hastens with his feet."*—reminds us being hasty with a decision is a sin, so given the size of the opportunity or potential for loss, you should spend enough time to make an informed decision. Become prepared and use your provisions.

Forsaking Yourself Anyhow

That is not to say that sometimes you will forsake yourself and God's provisions and plans. I can look back on numerous decisions I made all on my own for what seemed like great opportunities that turned out to be losses greater than I could afford at that time. To name a few examples, I borrowed money for cars I couldn't afford, I made purchases on credit cards when I should have used cash, and I bought a house when I was nineteen on a contract for deed. I bought into numerous "make-money" ideas, such as selling water purifiers back in the early 1980s when few people really cared about purified water. The borrowed money and credit cards cost me interest I couldn't afford. I didn't have a viable or sustainable income, so I had to walk away from the house and down payment I had made. After buying my inventory, I pretty much gave away the ugly countertop water purifiers. At that time, those opportunities seemed to be necessary or desirable to get ahead financially or to save money by buying now. Although they seemed necessary, they were only desirable. A trusted spouse, friend, or advisor could have easily pointed me in a better direction had I only shared my desire with them. Hindsight has demonstrated that I would have actually been further ahead today had I never pursued those desires.

Listening well, staying on God's task, and preparing thoroughly for that assignment can help you become less likely to take some fishy bait. It all comes down to how you move forward.

So how do you know when you're acting from desire, when you're taking bait you should leave alone? What if you have acquired lots of knowledge or advice from others? What if your decision is not being made in haste? What if everything—even prayer—seems to say, "Move forward"?

Well, if legally and ethically you can make a step forward, if that step is in your best interest *as well as for others involved*, then take that step only if you—and the others involved—can afford to take that calculated loss. Better yet, add some cushion to your calculated loss just in case your figures are off. The Lord never said that we would never suffer a loss: He said He wouldn't forsake us. If the calculated risk is what you and the others involved can afford to risk and lose, then if you do lose it, you will not be forsaken, you will not suffer much loss, your family will not suffer much, and others involved will not suffer much loss.

In his book *Think and Grow Rich,* Napoleon Hill put it this way, *"I fully realize that no wealth or position can long endure unless built upon truth and justice; therefore, I will engage in no transaction that does not benefit all whom it affects."*

Hill's statement is founded in Biblical truth: Righteousness and justice are the foundation of the Lord's throne (see Psalm 97:2). Truth, righteousness, and justice are important to the Lord. Acting in truth is sincerity in action and character. Righteousness—acting in accord with divine or moral law—helps you live free from guilt and sin. Justice is really not much more than being fair according to the rules of law. It shouldn't be an issue, but the tricky part for some people is considering "Whose law?"

Can you think of bait in your past that has tempted you, enticements or traps that have lured you into uncomfortable situations? Have you made unwise and poor investments? Perhaps you placed your trust in the wrong people Perhaps you stepped out of your calling and found yourself to be prey to some predator. Can you think of times when seeking advice would have been time well spent?

Watch who you listen to: Be careful around wealthy people who may use you in their schemes (see Proverbs 23:1–3). Likewise, watch what you say: It could get you into trouble (see Ephesians 4:29). Guard your mouth and tongue to keep yourself out of trouble (see Proverbs 21:23). Listening well, staying on God's task, and preparing thoroughly for that assignment can help you become less likely to take some fishy bait. It all comes down to how you move forward.

Chapter 3

Casting Off on the Voyage

Incline your ear and hear the words of the wise, and apply your heart to my knowledge...

Proverbs 22:17

He who has an ear, let him hear what the Spirit says...

Revelation 3:13

No temptation has overtaken you except such as is common to man; but God is faithful, who will not allow you to be tempted beyond what you are able, but with the temptation will also make the way of escape, that you may be able to bear it.

1 Corinthians 10:13

We got to his cabin and there the old pontoon boat rested on several cut logs. This pontoon boat was made of thick steel. It had heavy-gauge welded steel-

64

mesh panels on all four sides to keep riders safely onboard. The sides were firmly bolted, welded, and rusted to a steel platform that was securely welded to two long steel pontoon floats. I had seen less steel when I was sightseeing at Alcatraz, I thought to myself.

You know that feeling you get when you do not want to tell someone what you really feel? I had that feeling. I wondered, "What did I get myself into?" (from "The Parable of the Pontoon Boat")

"What did I get myself into?" Notice the past tense of the verb in that sentence? I hadn't yet gotten into trouble but I already thought it was too late. It wasn't too late. I just wasn't listening to the Holy Spirit. *"You know that feeling you get...?"* That feeling is the Holy Spirit telling you to take a "time out." Do not ignore the Holy Ghost. This is your chance to find the way of escape.

Jesus himself frequently said, *"He who has an ear to hear...."* Pay attention. Life is always better when you listen to Jesus. To be ignorant is to be destitute of knowledge, uninstructed, or un-informed. To be really ignorant is to purposely avoid seeking knowledge. Proverbs 2:11-12 tells us, *"Discretion will preserve you; understanding will keep you, to deliver you from the way of evil..."*

There is plenty of warning for those with an ear to hear. In the book of Acts (see chapter 27), Paul's voyage to Rome begins on an imperial grain ship. The *"winds were contrary"*— there's the warning: Don't go. The sailing was slow and difficult. There's another warning: Turn back or stop, find a place to temporarily anchor, and get your bearings. The voyage even became dangerous. Hello! Do you hear me?!...All right, have it your way! In verse 10, Paul advised them, *"Men, I perceive that this voyage will end with disaster and much loss...."*

The centurion from Julius who was aboard, however, was more persuaded by the ship's helmsman (its pilot) and owner. He had more trust in the voice of men than in the voice of God speaking through Paul. Instead of heeding the warning, just as we often do, the seamen ignored the warning signs and continued on their journey. Heads up, this is when things get worse before they get better. Shortly thereafter, they encountered a storm and were *"exceedingly tempest-tossed."* Now knowing what they were up against, they prepared for the worst and frapped the boat, *"used cables to undergird the ship,"* wrapping the cables around the hull and making them tight. Once we open our eyes to the truth, we prepare for the worst of the storm. Now our senses are working!

If you don't give up, if you obtain victory through your adversity by walking in faith and listening to God, you will come out with a higher level of authority and power to help build the Kingdom of God.

After abstaining from food, after time had passed, and after an angel visited Paul and gave him a message, Paul had the audacity to tell these Roman professional sailors in verse 21 and 22, *"Men, you should have listened to me...and now I urge you to take heart, for there will be no loss of life among you, but only of the ship...."* In other words, the ship is going down, but you will live.

Paul then took bread and gave thanks to the Lord in their presence. In the midst of the storm, in this terrible tempest, Paul took time to thank his Lord—and he did this in the presence of his enemies. What if they had thought Paul was mocking them? They might have thrown Paul overboard! Even though the others aboard were not walking in faith, Paul had incredible faith in his Lord. The next day, nearer to land, they all jumped overboard and were shipwrecked on the island of Malta.

Despite the warning signs, they hadn't listened, they proceeded anyhow, they faced worse circumstances and adversity than they imagined, and at least Paul walked by faith for them all to make it through.

And what is the message for you and me? At the onset, your ship and supplies are intact. After the "storm of adversity," you are left alive, but your ship and provisions are greatly jeopardized or may be lost altogether. If you don't give up, if you obtain victory through your adversity by walking in faith and listening to God, you will come out with a higher level of authority and power to help build the Kingdom of God.

My Nevada Storm Clouds Gather

You might recall that after meeting with the real estate investment expert and Jesse my client in Las Vegas, I created the limited liability company (LLC) fairly quickly. Weeks later, though, I started thinking more about the situation. Questions came to mind. What if someone thinks I not only originated loans for Jesse but was also doing this for myself? What if the LLC was believed to be more than shell? These "what ifs" could have severe consequences.

My gut rose to my throat. I realized that the fantasy in my mind had come to an end. Even if Jesse did want to bless me, as a banker I couldn't accept it. It would be wrong for many reasons. In fact, some people would believe that what I did even to this point was wrong or unethical. How could I be so ignorant, so gullible? Did I allow my trust to cloud my better judgment?

Looking back, I was caught up in the moment and I didn't want to tell him "no." Jesse had a powerful personality. He could be intimidating when angry. I had seen Jesse during real estate closings at title companies and he would use intimidation and other tactics to get his way. To be fair, I have seen other investors at real estate closings also use these intimidation tactics too. In any event, though, I didn't want to hurt Jesse's feelings by rejecting what seemed to be a gracious offer. I also didn't want to upset a client.

I decided I had to meet Jesse. He had to know that, despite his best wishes, I couldn't accept his "blessing." I had to tell Jesse that as a banker it would be wrong for me to be involved. My involvement would be considered self-serving and a serious conflict of interest. If someone actually thought I was part of this investment, I could have violated bank laws and regulations. Easy enough, I would tell Jesse that I could not accept any blessing, and whatever we thought we were going to do with the LLC, we couldn't.

As I mentioned, Jesse, like many wealthy individuals, had a powerful personality. I was concerned how he would react to what I had to say. In my most gracious and diplomatic way, I explained, "Jesse, this situation could appear very bad for me if someone drew the wrong conclusions. Someone might think I violated banking regulations."

Giving my very best heartfelt explanation and sharing my deepest concerns regarding my career, I went on to say, "If regulators actually thought I was a co-investor or could profit from a transaction in which I was also the lender, the consequences for me would be devastating."

Jesse had the audacity to say, "No, you are still in!"

In? What was I in? All we had was a verbal conversation and a LLC shell. Up to this point, although intimidating at times, Jesse had always shown himself to be a man of reason, at least with me. By his reaction, I realized that we were no longer sailing on the same boat; we were navigating different seas. I didn't exactly know why, but I felt duped and I didn't know what to say.

I left our meeting, leaving the LLC documentation with him and trusting he would do the right thing. I had figured he would either close the LLC or release my name from the organization documents if he wanted to keep the LLC open. Once the LLC was open and registered with the state, it would take both signatures—Jesse's and mine—to eliminate me from the LLC. It had become obvious from our conversation that Jesse wasn't going to oblige.

In the long run, I figured that Jesse could not make me receive money, so even if he kept the LLC with my name on it, in time this would just go away. "Jesse still cannot make me accept money," I told myself. "Just let this take its course and it will eventually die and go away. If he sells the units, I will just not accept anything. That will be easy."

A Deep Pit Is Revealed to Me

When storms along craggy coastlines threaten your voyage, look for the lighthouse to help guide you. That lighthouse is Christ!

More time passed. The 2006 market for selling these housing units was softening—their values were no longer climbing and fewer buyers were interested. Some investment analysts didn't think the market would rebound too fast. Jesse asked me if I knew of anyone who might be interested in his investment. Would anyone be willing to take over the purchase agreement based on the original 2005 pricing? The 2005 pricing still seemed to be a fair deal at that time.

As a banker, I knew many people, including a few people who were interested. These potential buyers were wealthy investors in commercial real estate properties and already owned rental units. Eventually a buyer was found. She signed a document that would transfer the real estate at closing. From what I remember this would save Jesse an assignment fee with the developer (seller).

When Jesse had contacted me about this, I realized I was still in a battle, and I pressed into the Lord. I looked for direction every step of the way. I paid careful attention to every dream I had and considered those that seemed to give me forewarning. These I now heeded.

In other words, when storms along craggy coastlines threaten your voyage, look for the lighthouse to help guide you. That lighthouse is Christ!

In one dream, the Lord showed me a very narrow path. It was a dangerous path across the top of a narrow mountain ridge, with steep slopes on both sides. Before me on this path, the Lord showed me a hidden pit, a trap concealed with straw as though meant to trap an animal. If I took one more step, I would fall into this deep pit. I noticed that Kristin was on the other side of this pit. Somehow she had made it around the pit and was still on this narrow path. The dream ended, but I knew that if I were careful, I could also make my way around the deep pit.

Later that afternoon I was with Jesse in his office sitting across from him at his large desk. Was it my perception or was my cushy leather chair lower than his? He presented legal documents to me and expected me to sign them right then and there. I would not be allowed to take them with me to review or seek counsel and advice.

Yes, you guessed it—these documents involved the LLC. The document used to assign the townhome was between the LLC and buyer, not between Jesse and the buyer. In other words, Jesse would need to first transfer the real estate purchase agreement to the name on the LLC before it could be sold through that LLC to the new buyer. One problem for him was that LLC still had my name on it. I would first have to be removed as one of the owners prior to closing, because as long as my name remained on the LLC, I would not agree to transfer any real estate into the LLC, much less out.

Remembering my dream that morning, I realized that this was the trap, the deep pit. "This was what my attorney said had to be done," I recall him saying as he reclined with his legs crossed, his feet up on his desk, and his arms and hands crossed behind his head. I would say that his body language was also telling me much! Despite his command to sign them, I gently placed the documents back on his desk. I didn't sign them. Praise God for speaking though dreams! Given that I hadn't signed the documents, I was surprised that he didn't say anything as I left his office.

Concealed Pitfalls

Not all traps and snares are obvious—most are intentionally concealed in some manner. The snare of the devil is a trap that has been set. This trap was made clear because the Lord revealed it to me in a dream. I am listening now!

"...My ears You have opened..." exclaims David in Psalm 40:6. The *MacArthur's Study Bible* (page 1913) explains that Greek translators regarded Hebrew words as figures of speech in which a part of something represented the whole. In this case, ears as organs of reception of God's Word represent obedience. Thus, hollowing ears open was part of the total work of fashioning a whole human body.

How many traps have been revealed to you in your life? Did you listen and heed the advice given to you by someone wiser, or did you allow yourself to be enticed into disaster and much loss? Did your boat survive or were you exceedingly tempest-tossed? Worse, were you taken captive? Were you asked to surrender? Or did you hear and receive the Word and escape whole?

It remains foolish to drift, though, when you are capable of plotting a course, making adjustments, and reaching familiar destinations.

From my own experiences, I can say I should have learned from previous situations so I would have recognized the next trap. Unfortunately, even when I have identified and learned from one situation, I didn't always recognize the next trap—and I haven't always been wise enough to step around it.

My nature is to be helpful, to help my clients reach their financial goals. It was very often the mission or vision of the banks where I worked. You might say that my nature and those banks' mission and values went hand in hand—sometimes too well.

If you like me, have found yourself teetering on the brink of some deep traps, this may be a great time to write out your circumstances or personality traits that are causing you difficulties and seek wise counsel. A wise counselor would be one knowledgeable of your type of circumstances. The advisor is probably not your best friend or neighbor. Again, be careful about whom you approach.

What traits do you have that can be both positive and negative? Do you always do what is in your best interest? Once you make a bad decision, have you noticed how much harder it is to avoid falling into the pit or hitting the rocky shore? Unfortunately, even when we use our best judgment, we can encounter circumstances that are difficult or even overwhelming. What started as someone who was going to bless me became a curse as well as a nightmare. Accepting a rusty old but free pontoon boat, and later the effort to get rid of that pontoon boat, paled in comparison but was so similar!

> *And that they may come to their senses and escape the snare of the devil, having been taken captive by him to do his will.*
>
> 2 Timothy 2:26

In the housing investment deal, I took the bait and ate it. Despite the obvious, I moved forward in my voyage and made the wrong decision. The obvious approach, in this case, would be to at least ask questions and more thoroughly understand what Jesse was offering me. I was not using all my senses at that time. My bearings were off. Too bad for me that I didn't stop to anchor and realign my bearings. Instead, I allowed myself to drift into dangerous waters. I accepted the idea of receiving Jesse's blessing without knowing what he really meant. I didn't ask any questions. I was afraid that questioning his seemingly gracious offer would offend him. And maybe his offer was gracious. Maybe he didn't anticipate the downside either. It remains foolish to drift, though, when you are capable of plotting a course, making adjustments, and reaching familiar destinations.

A fool is one who is unwise or imprudent and acts without judgment or discretion. Don't be foolish. If you need to drop anchor and reassess, do it. Listen to wise council and take time to replot your course.

Saying "No" Nicely?

You can be nice and say no, can't you? I didn't think so.

How many times have you wanted to say "no" but you didn't? Were you afraid it would hurt someone's feelings? Were you afraid of rejection? Did you think you would be thrown out of a group? For many years, it was my nature to be so nice that I wouldn't rock the boat. I would try to maintain peace at all costs. Some may see that as a desirable trait. Because of my own self-imposed insecurity, I was afraid of rejection and, in the end, truth was compromised. In short, I wanted the approval of "man." At times, I misunderstood approval for respect. Have you made that mistake?

Don't mistake being nice with doing what is right. Even if someone does get upset with you, it doesn't justify doing what is
wrong.

Pay now; later is more expensive. This is not about borrowing
money today to buy that boat on clearance or you will pay more
next year when the new models are more expensive. In my case,
had I said "no" right away (pay now), at the very worst, Jesse
would have ridiculed me for not taking advantage of a great opportunity, and maybe he would have taken his business elsewhere.
He may have been offended and rejected me, but I would not
have jeopardized my integrity or career. I paid a much larger price
than necessary. In contrast, let's see how Daniel handled bad
news with King Nebuchadnezzar.

King Nebuchadnezzar (1) by Mark Kuhne

Daniel had his hands full with King Nebuchadnezzar. One day under extreme consequences Daniel and his friends Shadrach, Meshach, and Abed-Nego were promoted after making known and interpreting King Nebuchadnezzar's first dream. A short time later, the king had them all bound and thrown in a fiery furnace for not bowing down to an idol, a gold image. God delivered them from the furnace and the king promoted them again (see Daniel 2-4, author paraphrase).

The schizophrenic king had yet another dream. Daniel, astonished, had to tell the king the terrible interpretation. Daniel essentially said, "Bad news! You're going to wallow in the mud like a beast. You'll be grazing grass until you tell God you're sorry! You'd better do the right thing right now or else!"

King Nebuchadnezzar (2) by Mark Kuhne

We know that Daniel lived to interpret dreams for Nebuchad-nezzar's son, Belshazzar, so we know that however Daniel told the dream and interpretation, he spoke the truth in love—and had the Lord's protection. Despite delivering bad news, Daniel forged ahead, risked his life, and was called back to interpret more dreams. The point is, kindly tell the truth, maintain your integrity, say or do what is right, and you will likely be respected, not rejected. Even if you are rejected, you've done the right thing. Ephesians 4:15 exhorts us to *"speak the truth in love"* with maturity so it doesn't sound cold.

The Cost? 25 Years

Avoiding delivery of difficult or bad news to save one's face comes in different packages. Remember, what you think you may have saved is nothing compared to your cost in the long run.

I remember a time in junior high school when I felt pressured to smoke cigarettes to be accepted into a group. Most of the ninth-graders had had three years or more to development friends and groups. In contrast, I had little over a month. Our family had moved to Redlands, California, during the last week of April, just five weeks before the end of that school year.

On my arrival at school I was assigned a student whose role was to introduce me around the campus. During lunch she escorted me to the outskirts of the athletic field to have lunch with her group. Several were smoking cigarettes and asked her if I was "cool." It was their way of asking whether I would reveal that they were smoking cigarettes on campus. She hardly knew me, so I quickly decided to demonstrate that I was cool without thinking about the consequences. The only consequence I saw at that moment was rejection by that group. I had never smoked cigarettes before, but I was afraid that if I didn't smoke a cigarette right then I would have been ostracized on my first day on campus. Obviously there were other students and groups I could have found and joined. I was afraid, however, to tell that group the truth. I went from an athletic group in Calabasas, California, to the smoking and "dope" group in Redlands.

During my high school years, I was arrested for being in the presence of illegal drugs. The drugs were not mine, but I was essentially guilty by association: I was with a classmate who had drugs in her purse. We were at the beach. The police suspected something, questioned us, and found the drugs. That arrest put my parents through agony. I also had to get permission from the school board to reenter school. Ultimately, choosing to smoke a cigarette that day cost me more than twenty-five years of smoking before I quit.

Speaking the Truth in Love

They didn't have Monster drinks then but even if they did, I doubt that the devil would have offered Him a drink.

We all know that Jesus was a master at speaking the truth in love. Jesus didn't compromise truth to prevent people from being offended:

79

- He denounced the Pharisees for their self-righteousness (see Matthew 23:33).
- Jesus turned over the tables of the money changers because their intentions were misaligned (see John 2:13–22).
- He told at least one person to let the dead bury their own dead (see Luke 9:59–60).

Jesus loved people enough to speak the truth (see Matthew 15:13–14). Jesus obeyed His Father's will and didn't assert His own rights. In doing so, however, He often offended many.

As another example, most people are familiar the scene when Jesus—being alone—meets a Samarian woman at the well (see John 4:5–42). He asked her for a drink. She knew Jesus as a Jew and questioned why He would even ask her for a drink, much less be in her presence. Jesus moved the conversation from the natural (asking for water) to the spiritual (talking about "living" water"). He then zeroed in on her sin: He told her that she had five husbands. He engaged her in conversation in such a way that she listened and was not offended. Instead, she went back to her city and invited many to the well to meet Jesus.

Even after being led into the wilderness with nothing to eat and being tempted for forty days by the devil (see Luke 4:2), Jesus spoke the truth kindly. The Bible says "He was hungry" (verse 2). The devil asks Jesus to turn a stone into bread. Jesus says, *"It is written, 'Man shall not live by bread alone, but by every word of God'"* (Luke 4:4). Does that sound like an angry, impatient response to you?

There is Jesus, hungry, tired, being told to turn stones into bread, the devil traipsing Jesus up a mountain, probably the rough and steep side too, and Jesus gave him one kind answer after another. I do not know the terrain in that wilderness, but it was likely difficult to walk. There could have been tree roots and rocks to circumvent. Maybe His neck and back were sore from sleeping on the ground for forty nights. His blood sugar may have been low from the lack of food. I imagine His energy dropped. They didn't have Monster drinks then but even if they did, I doubt that the devil would have offered Him a drink.

No. Instead, the devil offered Jesus a stone! Wouldn't you be offended if a waiter at a restaurant presented you a stone on a plate after you had been waiting longer than usual for your meal? Again, Jesus says, *"It is written, 'Man shall not live by bread alone, but by every word of God.'"* Mind you, Jesus was talking to the devil! Jesus had every right to be mean, didn't He? The devil is His enemy. The devil is against Him. It was not until the devil suggested Jesus worship him and *"...all will be Yours,"* that Jesus said to him, *"...Get behind Me, Satan...!"* with an exclamation point (Luke 4:7-8). Don't ask me what I would say if you took me to the pinnacle of a tall temple and told me to jump. But there is Jesus calmly telling him, *"...You shall not tempt the Lord your God"* (Luke 4:12).

I know what I am like when my children pester me for just one day. Whether I am hungry or not, after several hours I struggle to remain patient and kind. I am fortunate that they are obedient and good 99.9 percent of the time. With respect to being hungry, deprive me of food for several hours and I can get a bit owly. Don't stand between me and my next meal! My blood sugar drops (or I think it does) and I struggle to be kind. I just want the food and I want it now.

Once, after waiting thirty to forty minutes after ordering our meal at a pizza place, I learned that our order had been given to another table. Had I not asked the waitress about our food, we might have waited more than an hour. No one told us anything about our order. I had to inquire. Naturally they offered to resubmit the order, but I had no desire to wait any longer to eat. I practically grabbed my family from their seats and walked them across the lot to a fast food Mexican restaurant.

Later I felt bad, because I learned from my wife that the waitress had just started that day. Even so, I am not sure I could have waited any longer to be fed. In that case I spoke the truth to the waitress about being unhappy about our order, but I didn't speak in love. Jesus probably would have taken the time to understand her situation and offered to help bus her tables.

Learning from Our History

We have all heard the saying to "never look a gift horse in the mouth." I suggest that you not only look deeply in the horse's mouth, but also inspect the horse's bones!

Truth is not about moving forward or holding back, anchoring or setting sail, but about assessing your situation and doing what is right so you and your crew and your boat get to your destination without injury or insult. Know yourself, know your skills and abilities, determine your passion in life, understand your level of authority, and act within your means.

Daniel moved ahead by doing the right thing, even when it meant conveying bad news. Jesus didn't do what the devil was telling Him to do. Jesus did the right thing; He was being obedient to the will of His Father. Jesus did not feed His flesh with food or with the power offered to him by the devil.

When is the last time you fed your flesh? What was your motivation? Greed? Envy? Pleasure? Did it feel good while it lasted? What about later? Have you developed ways to say "no" to yourself? Peer pressure is one thing, but we apply self-pressure too. I love sporting goods stores, as well as car and boat dealerships, but I remind myself that cannot have everything I see and desire.

Are you capable of giving God the helm? How do know you can trust God to help you? Proverbs 18:10 says, *"The name of the Lord is a strong tower; the righteous run to it and are safe."* In other words, if we open our ears to Him, if we give God the helm, if we look to him as our lighthouse, we will be safe.

How do we make sure we have an ear opened to hear? The pain of a memory may keep me from make the same mistake twice, but what if I am facing a situation for the first time? My history teachers said we should study history to understand it to avoid making mistakes in the future. I didn't care for this reason to study history, but they made a valid point: We can learn by the mistakes (and successes) of others. For instance, you can read your Bible every day to learn ways to steer your boat in the right direction. (The book of Proverbs is an excellent place to start! In fact, there are 31 chapters in Proverbs—you could read one each day.)

With respect to the free pontoon boat offer and Jesse's offer to be blessed, I had the ability to reject both. I could have listened and learned from my own history, and I could have answered differently. When I saw the pontoon boat, it clearly was not what I had had in mind. My gut was screaming, "No, no, no, don't take it!" But I didn't listen, and as soon as we winched the boat onto the trailer I had rented, I knew the problem had become mine.

Jesse's offer of a blessing wasn't so easy for me to see. It was intangible and vague. Further, did he really intend to share his upside with me? On one hand I didn't think the blessing was any obligation on my part and I made it clear I had no money in his investment. On the other hand, I didn't ask any detailed questions because I feared his response. At the time of the offer, I did not consider what Jesse's blessing meant. I could have said to Jesse, "I appreciate your offer to bless me, but before I accept your offer, let me think more about it. When you return to Minnesota we can talk more." In other words, I could have given myself more time.

We have all heard the saying to "never look a gift horse in the mouth." I suggest that you not only look deeply in the horse's mouth, but also inspect the horse's bones! In other words, check the structure of your boat to determine whether it will handle the seas you plan to sail! Don't be fooled by offers that appear to be free or inexpensive. Don't be afraid of the response when you reject someone's offer. In the next chapter we will look deeper at overlooking the obvious and making bad decisions.

Chapter 4

Navigating Badly

> *...My son, do not walk in the way with them, keep your foot from their path; for their feet run to evil... they lurk secretly for their own lives. So are the ways of everyone who is greedy for gain; it takes away the life of its owners.*
>
> Proverbs 1:15-16, 18-19

That's right—I had spent another $10 on lunch. I envisioned cash flying out of my wallet as I figured out what it might cost to get this behemoth in the water as a swim platform. Oh well, if nothing else, I could junk it.... *This was my problem now. What an eyesore!* (from "The Parable of the Pontoon Boat")

"This was my problem now." Why had I moved forward? Why did I justify all this trouble? Why do any of us move forward, overlook the obvious, and take the bait, eat the fruit? Are we looking for acceptance? Perhaps we are afraid of confrontation at the risk of losing acceptance with a friend, co-worker, or acquaintance. Is *acceptance* at the root of giving control and trust to the wrong people? Is it our inner need or desire to be loved? Does our

desire for acceptance *by man* result in us allowing a controlling spirit over us?

Or is our desire for the things we want that God has not yet granted us what opens the door for Satan to sneak into our lives, to steer our boat? Isn't this just a form of selfishness?

A pontoon boat was something I wanted. I didn't have a pontoon boat at the cabin. I didn't want to wait any longer for a pontoon boat. Because I didn't wait for God's timing, my foolishness or dissatisfaction, my not waiting for the right time clouded my judgment and invited trouble. Proverbs 19:23 puts it like this: *"The fear of the Lord leads to life, and he who has it will abide in satisfaction; he will not be visited with evil."* Granted, getting rid of the old rusty pontoon boat was a small consequence compared with other foolish decisions I have made to want or have something before God wanted me to have it—foolish decisions that resulted in much larger consequences.

I didn't want to wait any longer for something I had convinced myself I needed, something I desired. I didn't want to wait for God's timing. Being selfish, impatient, being foolish, caused me to give birth to a Big Problem. You could say I gave birth to an "Ishmael." (Have you ever given birth to an "Ishmael"?)

Sound familiar? We all know the story about Sarai and Abram, who had yet to bear any children. The Lord God himself told Abram in Genesis 15:5, *"Look now toward heaven, and count the stars if you are able to number them...So shall your descendants be."*

After ten childless years, Sarai felt that the Lord had restrained her from having any children. Who wouldn't after ten years? To anyone wanting children, ten years would seem like an eternity. It seemed like a good time to help God get these descendants started! So, given the custom of that day in which a barren wife would use one of her maidservants to get a child, and with Abram yielding to sin—ignoring God's divine assurance— Ishmael was born through Hagar the maidservant. In other words, an "Ishmael" was born. This was a Big Problem! (In fact, it has not gone away to this day....) Once Ishmael was born, he came with a warning tag: *"He shall be a wild man; his hand shall be against every man..."* (Genesis 16:12).

Consider Abram—can you see Abram standing outside late at night, far away from his tent, far away from Sarai and Hagar, his arms and hands are stretched to the heavens, his face is looking up at all the stars searching for God, and in a loud voice of despair, he essentially says, "Great! Now you tell me! Lord, how come Your divine assurance didn't tell me exactly *how* and *when* my descendants would be started? Lordy, Lordy...oh what have I done this time! Oh, I am too old for this. Woe is me!" Realizing his bad choice and the great trouble before him, realizing that once you start a Big Problem it does not easily go away, mumbling to himself, he slowly makes his way home, possibly curses at a tree or two, kicks a few stones along the way, quietly enters his tent, crawls onto his blanket, and prays himself to sleep.

Does this sound familiar to you? Have you ever driven your car the long way home, cursed at a few cars and billboards along the way, mumbled about what to do next, quietly entered your home, fell into bed, and prayed yourself to sleep?

Making the Wrong Turn

Once his money was invested in that scheme, it was as good as gone.

Here's how a friend described his "Ishmael" story to me:

"I had everything in place; I spent my working lifetime setting up my business. I had assets that were paid for and a good cash flow. I wanted to retire early and was open to other investments that could get me there more quickly. I was out of my area of expertise, vulnerable, and gullible to those I trusted. I was open to being lured. So I used my entire base of cash and investments that took a lifetime to acquire and made wrong decisions. Everyone should have a base of cash that they do not touch. They should protect their hard-earned investments so they are never wiped out or made vulnerable. I am starting over."

Prepare your outside work, make it fit for yourself in the field; and afterward build your house.

Proverbs 24:27

My friend did exactly as the Bible taught in Proverbs: He built his business (prepared his work) and a financial base (made it fit) and he established a base of investments (built his house) so that he was secure. What went wrong? He cut corners to obtain an earlier retirement. He took 100 percent of his liquidity—his cash and investments—and invested poorly into what turned out to be a scheme. Once his money was invested in that scheme, it was as good as gone.

Once I had the pontoon boat on the trailer, I was committed. Once you step over the "line," you will generally keep going… at least for a while. That little while can hurt a lot. Sometimes it is the "speed" at which you are moving. That speed is called momentum. There is "mass" behind momentum. That pontoon boat had plenty of mass! Most often, however, the weight is in our heads. In your head, you have committed to a bad direction, and one step is followed by another because your head hasn't said "stop!" Even when your head and mouth say "stop," it may take more effort to bring things to a halt. Engineers driving trains and captains steering barges must make decisions long in advance to control the train or barge. The more weight your vehicle carries, the longer it may take to bring things under your control.

How Do We Plot a Direct Course?

What can you do today to help guide your future decisions, in fact, to shape your future? To start, it helps to know the principles that will guide you. A boat on a small lake and a barge on the ocean are guided by similar but different standards. Identify your principles or standards that shape your values, morality, and mission. Determine what is nonnegotiable for you.

My standard is the Bible: I use it to predetermine answers to issues that may or may not arise sometime in my future. I have written a vision statement for myself and my family. My wife and I update our vision statement annually. The more you can identify what you want your future to look like and plan how to get there, the better you will be at staying the course.

Tacking toward a destination is one thing, but thoughtlessly or unconsciously changing directions or drifting may lead to raging waters.

Every sailor knows that the quickest way to get from point A to point Z is a straight line, but given wind, currents, storms, and other factors, sailors almost always have to tack or zigzag to stay the course. Tacking toward a destination is one thing, but thoughtlessly or unconsciously changing directions or drifting may lead to raging waters. As another example, when I'm fishing with my friend Ray in Florida, I know he will not motor his fourteen-foot fishing boat any farther from where he can see the shoreline. Ray knows that his boating skills are best used in the calmer gulf waters—closer to shore—where he can constantly see land. He knows his skills and abilities and stays true to them. Do you?

Knowing your standards, and staying true to them, prepares you for future situations. You have plotted your course and have a pretty good idea how to get there. Decisions then are measured against that plotted course you've planned, rather than being swayed by the lure of desire.

I wanted a pontoon boat. It was in my plan to have one. It was not in my plan to own a massive rusted chunk of steel. I should have noticed that this vessel, while shaped like a pontoon boat, wasn't going to float and behave like a pontoon boat. I should have never put it on the trailer. I should have said, "Thanks, I know I told you over the phone I would take it, and here I am with the trailer, but I didn't realize this had so much rust. I am not prepared to fix this and cannot accept your offer."

Instead, I concocted some reason—rationalized—to accept the boat to maintain my relationship with the broker. I also thought I would be going against my word because I had told him I would take it. On the other hand, he had told me it was seaworthy. I made a decision without looking at the boat because it was "free." It would have been wiser to look and properly analyze the situation—assessed whether it fit in my plan and matched my standards—before I made the decision.

Jesse's offer seemed free too, but in a way it was invisible: I couldn't see and touch it the way I could a rusty old boat. Having been a commercial banker for more than twenty-five years, I have reviewed and financed numerous real estate loan requests. Aside from buying a personal residence, investing in real estate was foreign to me, outside my previous experiences. Jesse specifically told me I wouldn't need to invest any capital, but I should have at least asked for more time to consider his offer, his blessing. I didn't have a well-defined plotted course at that time: Whatever my vague plan was, it did not include offers like Jesse's.

Being in foreign waters, I should have anchored and got my bearings. Instead, I rationalized saying "yes" to Jesse to avoid appearing ungracious about his free offer, as well as for the reasons I mentioned earlier. My justification to accept his offer seemed reasonable but was unrelated to the real issue. My feelings, the potential loss of a client and thinking I would appear ungracious, for example, are not related to the truth that the Jesse's offer did not fit within my plans or standards. I wish I could say that the sun was in my eyes, but I have no one to blame but myself. I wasn't being true to myself. I wasn't staying my course and, whether consciously or unconsciously, I drifted into raging waters.

I don't know exactly what Sarai was thinking, but she rationalized a plan to help God fulfill Abram's dream to have a child. She didn't anticipate Hagar's contemptuous disregard. Genesis 16:4 states, *"So he went in to Hagar, and she conceived. And when she saw that she had conceived, her mistress became despised in her eyes."* The goal of having a child was understandable, but her plan was terrible and led to trouble.

Similarly, my desire for a pontoon boat was okay, but with the sun in my eyes (just kidding), I accepted the boat and created trouble for myself. My plan to be the best business banker for my clients was okay, but without sufficient analysis of Jesse's offer, I created a Big Problem for myself. By the time Jesse was demanding me to sign papers, my eyes were seeing very clearly!

Steering by the Charted Course

Employ lots of analysis for your high-risk decisions. Especially do not allow your trust of someone get in the way of your analysis.

I'm not only seeing more clearly—I also have a much clearer plan and course that I follow.

Because of my banking background, I was recently presented an opportunity to create and co-own a car-rental business with two to four rental cars in American Samoa. Considering that cars rent here at $100 a day and that supply is much less than demand, the opportunity looked good on the surface. I asked several questions over a few days and gave it some consideration, but in the end, I compared the opportunity to my plan, my plotted course. It didn't take long to figure out that co-owning a car-rental business would take me off my course and lead me to troubled waters. I know very little about cars or the car-rental business, I am not an accountant, I am not called to be an accountant or to run a car-rental company, and I am living in American Samoa for only a short period of time. How would I help manage the company when I return to the U.S. mainland?

Of course, there was much more to it than that, but you get the point. Not only was it outside my area of expertise; more importantly, it was not part of my plan. I even explained my reasons for my decision by explaining my past experiences. The local man hoping to open a car-rental company may not be pleased with me or my decision, but I didn't lose a friend. I was kind and truthful.

Ponder the path of your feet, and let all your ways be established.

Proverbs 4:26

My wife and I are serious about looking out on our horizon, pondering the path of our feet, and letting our ways be established. We have shared this concept with our two youngest daughters. While at our cabin one weekend, we asked the girls to grab paper and pens and to join us on the sun porch. The porch was our favorite place at the cabin because it sat high and looked out over the entire lake—a great location with wonderful perspective, like a crow's nest on an old sailing ship. We asked each of them to write out what their future husband would look like. Of course, they included physical features, but more importantly, their descriptions indirectly described values. Their descriptions are a secret with me, but suffice it to say that with much prompting from my wife and I, they created very detailed lists that describe not only what they want but also what they do not want in their husbands. Perhaps without realizing it, and admittedly with our prompting, they've begun charting a future course.

In my past, I didn't predetermine that when I was faced with a decision outside my area of expertise I would seek advice from an expert. I let the beauty of the fruit in my hand confuse me and I let myself be gullible. Don't make those mistakes. Employ lots of analysis for your high-risk decisions. Especially do not allow your trust of someone get in the way of your analysis. Like steering a barge, beware of small changes that can have big outcomes, whether good or bad.

Write out your plan and include what definitely will *not* be in your plan. How much will you have in savings one year from now, two years from now? How much debt will you accept and when will you be debt-free? What is the maximum amount of savings you will risk at any given time? As you reach age fifty-five or sixty-five, will your tolerance to risk change? How so? What will you do differently? Write it out. Tack along your course and anchor at times if you must to reconsider direction. Alter headings to stay the course, allow for changes to your destination after you weigh potential rewards against the consequences, and keep your eyes open for floating and submerged debris.

Do you have a place to seek perspective? Climb up to your crow's nest now and determine whether you are on track or lost.

What do you see?

Chapter 5

Beset by Ill Winds

> *...and suddenly a great wind came from across the wilderness and struck the four corners of the house, and it fell...*
>
> Job 1:19

> *But when he saw that the wind was boisterous, he was afraid; and beginning to sink he cried out, saying, "Lord, save me!"*
>
> Matthew 14:30

Even when you are savvy enough to have a charted course, even when you are obedient and follow the Lord's course, you'll be affected by your own character flaws/weaknesses, manipulators, and outright Jezebel spirits' pressure. Life has setbacks. Consider Joseph when he went to his brothers and they stripped him of his tunic: *"the tunic of many colors that was on him...then they took him and cast him into a pit"* (Genesis 37:23–24).

I was quietly upset and angry with myself for accepting this "free" pontoon boat. I was very quiet while I thought about what I was going to do what seemed like with several tons of steel in my yard. I think the boat sat taller than the cabin—it was certainly heavier. Yikes, what would my wife Kristin think when she sees this occupying our land? Maybe she wouldn't notice. (from "The Parable of the Pontoon Boat")

I was gullible, meandered off course, and allowed myself to drift into water more dangerous than I could navigate.

Lack of fear of the Lord is a lack of obedience in all things. If we fear the Lord, we will walk in integrity in all that we do. Proverbs 14 says, *"in the fear of the Lord there is strong confidence, and His children will have a place of refuge"* (verse 26), and you will *"...turn away from the snares of death"* (verse 27).

What part of my character allowed me to be foolish that I walked right into the snare of the "free" pontoon boat?

Character is explained many ways, but I like to think of character as what others see plus what we see in ourselves plus the God-given uniqueness within us. Others primarily determine their view of our character from our actions they witness or hear about filtered through their belief system or values and perception. In contrast, we often see ourselves based on our intentions (also filtered through our beliefs and values). We also have talents or skills (giftedness) that I believe are God-given and unique and shape and influence our character. I further believe that God gave us a unique giftedness to help others in ways that build the Kingdom of God. My character may be similar to someone else's, but it is also unique. The better you understand yourself, as well as your area of expertise, the better you can plot your course. So what part of my character led me to be foolish? I was gullible, meandered off course, and allowed myself to drift into water more dangerous than I could navigate.

In my Bible, Proverbs chapter 1 is titled "The Beginning of Knowledge." Solomon was known to be the wisest man in the world. He had much to say about wisdom, instruction, under-standing, prudence, discretion, learning, attaining wise counsel, and in verse 7, he says, *"The fear of the Lord is the beginning of knowledge, but fools despise wisdom and instruction."* The overriding theme of Proverbs is the fear of the Lord— in other words, admiration, submission, and reverence—is the foundation of knowledge and wisdom. Submission, by the way, is not blind in this case, but to come *under* (sub) God's *mission* (the Word):

> *"...fools hate knowledge"* (verse 22),

> *"They would have none of my counsel..."* (verse 30),

> *"Therefore they shall eat the fruit of their own way, and be filled to the full with their own fancies"* (verse 31),

> *"...the complacency of fools will destroy them..."* (verse 32).

In chapter 3 we read in verse 7, *"Do not be wise in your owns eyes; fear the Lord..."* and in verse 35 that *"shame shall be the legacy of fools."* Chapter 12, verse 15 teaches that *"The way of the fool is right in his own eyes, but he who heeds counsel is wise."* The Book of Proverbs says much about fools. The fool's mouth leads him toward destruction and his lips are a snare (see Proverbs 18:7). Ouch! I "resembled" that!

In my recent storms, I hadn't taken the time to gain knowledge and understanding. Without seeing the pontoon, I agreed to take it over a phone conversation. Without understanding what Jesse meant, I accepted his offer of a blessing. In both cases I ate the fruit of my own actions. In both cases I was led to problems, the latter being much bigger than the former. I was complacent in that I didn't analyze what *blessing* meant to Jesse and I misplaced my loyalty or trust in him. Likewise, I was complacent in that I didn't consider the consequences with respect to bank regulations, my bank position, or career. By being gullible (high trust, low analysis), I allowed my lips to say yes and become a snare.

The fear of man brings a snare, but whoever trusts in the Lord shall be safe.

Proverbs 29:25

What was wrong with my character? I was gullible! In particular, I was gullible with people I highly trusted. I was dissolute of discernment at the very moment I needed discernment most—not because it wasn't available to me, but because I misplaced my trust and loyalty to a person! In other words, I feared man, not the Lord. I was not safe and set on high. Contrarily, *"...the Lord will give grace and glory; no good thing will He withhold from those who walk uprightly. Oh Lord of hosts, blessed is the man who trusts in You"* (Psalm 84:11–12)!

> *From the end of the earth I will cry to You, when my heart is overwhelmed;*
> *lead me to the rock that is higher than I.*
>
> Psalm 61:2

I was also complacent by not analyzing the situations. Complacency is similar to cutting corners. Remember my friend in the last chapter who invested his entire lifetime of savings in an investment recommended to him by a trusted friend? There is that high trust and low analysis again! He desired to retire earlier and took what seemed to be an easier and faster way to building his retirement funds. Instead he lost everything. The investment turned out to be a scheme. He was questioned by the Federal Bureau of Investigation (FBI) to determine what part he played, if any, in the scheme. Thankfully, his part was only his investment. He is back on track today, but he lost his house and much more because he was complacent and lacked discernment.

Beware of Submerged Rocks along Shortcuts

Why do we cut corners or try to take what seems an easy or short route? How often do you find yourself wondering why you made that decision? What happened between point A and Z that got me into this trouble? Did I place too much trust in a "person" or in what I perceived to be the person's expertise? Was it greed or envy that led me into uncharted waters? What weaknesses in your character have led you toward trouble? Mind you, I have come to a point in my life that I have forsaken myself enough times and determined to put that to an end. Now that I have had plenty of experiences and gathered some wisdom, I am sharing this wisdom with you so you too can put an end to forsaking yourself.

Sometimes our trouble comes not because of our character or because we fell prey to an evil person but because we felt pressured or shamed into making a bad decision. I call that manipulation. Few characters exemplify manipulation better than Jezebel in the two books of Kings in the Bible. To this day she remains notorious for manipulation and many have written about her controlling nature. I imagine that some of you may think the following exchange sounds perfectly normal, and it may be. Others may sense the hair on their back rising and identified with Jeremiah's uneasiness over the situation and the timing. A few may actually feel Satan gripping Jeremiah's throat, his dagger piercing Jeremiah's heart, and his hand in Jeremiah's wallet. Some dialogue such Jezebel characters use to control and manipulate is more obvious than others. Some phrases or words may have rubbed you the wrong way but you had difficulty placing your finger on exactly why the words made you uneasy.

To respond truthfully, though, you must first have clear perception; your eyes must be opened.

Consider this situation that started with an e-mail. Within the messages that followed that first e-mail, I have highlighted certain words to bring them to your attention. Look at how Satan can orchestrate the spirit of control and manipulation in this spiritual battle that is not really about the siblings or their father. Obviously, the names and details were changed for legal and privacy reasons. In particular, to demonstrate the spiritual battle more clearly, I'm calling the people involved by the names Jezebel and Ahab, as well as Jeremiah and Aunt Beth. Although I use this exchange and these characters to illustrate a spiritual battle, the individuals' intentions may not have been evil. I think you get the picture.

Jezebel and Ahab by Mark Kuhne

Here's Jezebel's e-mail that began the discussion (the emphasis in "***bold***" is mine):

*"...lastly, there has been a discussion by **all of us** to **chip in** to pay off the rest of dad's debt, which would be about $3,000 each. When dad passes away, **we'd** split the sale of his house in thirds and **get that money back**. It would **help dad immensely**, as what he has to live on is **peanuts**.*

*I've spoken with Ahab and **we** are both committed to this, but I haven't heard directly from Jeremiah **if you are in**. If not, **we'll** have to figure out how to split the sale of his house **accordingly** when that time comes."*

So far only Jezebel and Ahab have discussed this proposition. Notice how she used words to lure her siblings. "Chipping in" suggested that it was as minimal as a couple of dollars. "Immensely" exaggerated and colored the situation being described. Likewise, "peanuts" was more color being used to manipulate. The reality was that their father didn't live on minimal income. Their father golfed frequently and he was considering replacing his clubs and making other plans. Don't misunderstand my point: It was the father's right to live as he pleased and to make these decisions without his children passing judgment on him. But I mention these details, these discrepancies, to show the context of the dialogue relative to the situation. This proposal was the first that Jeremiah had heard of it, but it wasn't worded as such. The manipulation implied that if you were not "in," you were not supporting your father, and you should be ashamed and guilty. "Accordingly" suggested the siblings were "out" if they did not go along.

Jeremiah responded, *"I cannot recall discussing this before. There are better ways to do this."*

Jeremiah was being nice but said in effect, "This is news to me! What are you talking about? Let's slow down and think this through."

Jeremiah continued with some options to consider:

*"(1) Aunt Beth keeps gifting dad and as long as Beth does that I would let dad apply those funds to his debt; (2) reverse mortgage that would pay him to live there if he has enough equity; (3) **if** I decided to help pay off his debt, I would want his house somehow deeded to an LLC with an **attorney** setting the ownership **very carefully** so we all are owners (including dad) but such that no additional debt can be placed against his house. Dad's ownership would be the value over and above our portions that we kick in as follows:*

- *have house appraised to established initial value*
- *$100,000 value (estimated for this example)*
- *Dad owns 91% ($91,000 equity)*
- *Jeremiah 3% ($3,000 cash)*
- *Ahab 3% ($3,000 cash)*
- *Jezebel 3% ($3,000 cash)*

*"It now has a stepped-up value and is held/owned in a LLC separate from a trust, will, estate, etc., and upon his death, his shares of the LLC could be distributed evenly between the remaining shareholders, etc. If dad was in a car accident (or something) and if he were sued, his equity would be protected also. That example is extremely **simplified**. Dad would pay "rent" to the LLC that is equal to property taxes and insurance so there is **no income or loss** from the LLC. The **lease term** would be **his lifetime** so he is **assured** of staying there. Are you sure dad only owes $9,000? We all have very different family, college, children and debt obligations. Obviously, there are other **possibilities to explore**."*

Jeremiah was trying to be prudent and suggested including an objective third-party expert.

It appears, though, that Jeremiah may have been sucked into the presumptuous position of making an estate decision without his father's input. Shame on Jeremiah—he had been doing pretty well in his initial response. Nonetheless, some thought and analysis went into Jeremiah's suggestions. He also acknowledged that the example wasn't totally considered and needed the help of an attorney. Jeremiah was not suggesting a shortcut at all, because this decision would affect each sibling very differently.

Jezebel responded quickly:

*"**Maybe** only **Ahab and I** discussed this, I **wasn't sure**. All **good points**, some **beyond my expertise**, but one thing I want to respond to is this: If dad's Aunt Beth continues to gift him, it will take about 3 years for dad to pay off his debt! Dad has **little to nothing to live on** after his $400/Mo debt payment, so I'd like to help him out **ASAP**. It would be a **small sacrifice** for **us** and a **HUGE benefit** to **his** daily life, but if it is beyond what **any single one of you wants** to do, then that's **of course your choice**. I do plan to help him and will want to make this happen in a **smooth legal manner**, so any suggestions as to how to proceed is appreciated, such as your LLC suggestion, Jeremiah. **I can** meet with a lawyer and get counsel, or **maybe we all** can together? I'm not sure of the exact amount, but I was taking into consideration that if Aunt Beth gifts dad this year, that would definitely cover what he owes along with our $9,000. In other words, I know it's not over $17,000, but the exact amount **eludes me now**."*

Jezebel tried to diminish Jeremiah's comment that "maybe" all were not included in this discussion, but hey, whatever. Also note how Jezebel pairs herself with Ahab. Watch out when you hear flattery: The devil is an expert at dialogue and strategically acknowledged that Jeremiah made "good points." Flattery is perverted praise (see Psalm 36:1–3). Don't be fooled: Jezebel stated that she lacked expertise and followed this with "but." She may lack expertise in this financial or legal matter, but she is clever in getting what she desires. Again she used exaggeration to color the situation. Just so you know, with Aunt Beth's next gift of approximately $5,000, their father could pay down his debt to $12,000, refinance at 6 percent and have a lower payment. The reverse mortgage would remain an option in the future, and their father's social security was also about to increase in a few months. This was not urgent as "ASAP" would suggest. And three to four years remaining to pay off one's debt is not dire straits. In separating herself from the "us," Jezebel was setting up an "oh, woe is me" reaction so the others would feel sorry, guilty, or ashamed for her to have to do this by herself. Can you hear the devil saying, "This won't really hurt; it will be smooth and legal"? Be cautious, for no-thing eludes the devil; it is the devil's purpose to elude, deceive, and confuse you.

Jezebel immediately wrote again without waiting for any response:

*"I didn't copy the others on my last e-mail. One correction...to rely on Aunt Beth's gifting, assuming it continues annually, would take about 3 years. Dad is **barely squeaking by**, so **let's chew** on an idea. **But...I don't want to get involved in some kind of tense situation** with this, so*

*if it looks like it will be **too complicated, I'll just** gift him **on my own** and **that will be that, come what may.***"

Previously, Jezebel had said that dad was "living on peanuts." Now he is "barely squeaking by." Jezebel's last sentence was the classic manipulation that often pulls the rug out from underneath the targeted person, leaving the person wondering what happened. So far the devil had suggested that Jeremiah go along with the plan or he will be left out. The devil implied that he will look like a loser if he does not support their father exactly the way the devil suggests. So far the devil has been on offense and Jeremiah has been on defense. Now the devil implied that Jezebel was the martyr: "*I don't want to create a tense situation…if it looks like it will be too complicated…I'll just…on my own…*" followed by the warning "*that will be that, come what may.*" The devil just made Jeremiah the offender, the attacker, and the devil pretended to be the victim, the martyr. You can be certain, there will be hell paid if the devil's manipulation and strategy doesn't work through Jezebel on Jeremiah.

Ahab finally disclosed his co-conspirator alliance:

"*Jezebel and I discussed that this would be **nice** and **really help dad** have a **nice retirement**. We were going to bring it up at **the meeting** but ran out of time. **Bottom line** is this. Dad owes $17,000. Aunt Beth most likely will gift him at the beginning of next year. Won't know until next year for sure. The **corporation** would be **very complicated and costly** as we would have to have tax returns and corporate filing expenses.*

*Bottom line is that we do all have different obligations and expenses. If Aunt Beth does gift him, **we all would have to** contribute about $3,000 each. **Not a lot** considering what we are going to receive but it would make a **huge difference** for him. Since we are all equal shareholders in **his estate** when the time comes **we would all get that back**. Albeit without interest but that would be **small potatoes** anyway. So **think about this** and then when dad knows what Aunt Beth does (**after the first of the year**) then we can **all** decide what is best for our individual situation and how **we** can (**or if you want to**) **help dad**."*

Much occurred in Ahab's e-mail, but let's concentrate on the bigger issues. Jezebel took a break and Ahab picked up the slack. What slack? There wasn't any slack. Ahab pushed forward the manipulation and drove home the guilt. Jeremiah never said it wouldn't be nice or that dad didn't deserve a nice retirement. Jeremiah doesn't care how his father uses his money: He doesn't see, however, the need to help him financially at this particular stage in his life. What is important about the "meeting" is that Jezebel and Ahab had already been discussing this but tried to make it look like all the siblings had been involved. The term "bottom line" indicates something final, like a fact that cannot be denied; corporate executives often use this term so it also has an air of authority.

Next Ahab suggested cutting corners. Ahab said a corporation will be "very complicated and costly." Note that Ahab confirmed and validated what Jezebel already said. In the Bible, Ahab is not known as a strong leader, because he goes along with Jezebel.

Jezebel leads; Ahab follows. Notice in my painting "Jezebel and Ahab" that Ahab is but a shadow within Jezebel's face (page 103). The devil in the garden to Eve said, *"...You will not surely die, will you?"* (Genesis 3:4). Speaking through Ahab in a similar way, the devil says, *"Giving dad $3,000 won't really hurt you; you will get it back."* But $3,000 may be a lot to some. And what's up with all the food terms? Now we have "small potatoes" to chew on besides peanuts. Just take a bite—it won't hurt you! Who was the "we" deciding what Jeremiah will spend? How were "all" going to decide what was best for their situations. Lastly Ahab twists the dagger of guilt deep into Jeremiah's heart with "(or if you want to) help dad." Ahab even placed it in parentheses! Feel guilty or help dad.

If you guessed this was a fight over the estate, you guessed wrong. This was not a fight over the distribution of the estate. It isn't even a fight. The dialogue had to do with a "suggestion" made by two of the siblings. This was not a battle against flesh and blood. It was also not about their father or his spending. He had the ability and right to spend and golf as he desired. This was an excellent example of what could be a spiritual battle in the heavenly realms.

This story was also an example of how pressure, guilt, and shame are used to manipulate a person into taking bait or navigating into the rocks. As you'll see in chapter 7, the best way to handle a Jezebel-like controlling person is with truth. Jezebel will likely twist and turn the conversation in several directions, but keep your responses to the point and grounded firmly in truth. To respond truthfully, though, you must first have clear perception; your eyes must be opened.

Chapter 6

Changing Direction

I started checking around to see whether floats could be replaced. It didn't take me long to learn that anything can be done—for a price. Given the cost, as well as the look on Kristin's face, I decided to trash the pontoon boat. Naturally, this proved to be easier said than done. This old pontoon boat had been around for a long time—maybe it was even used to float Washington's troops across the Potomac. Why did I think I could get rid of it quickly?
(from "The Parable of the Pontoon Boat")

> *Then the eyes of both of them were opened, and they knew that they were naked; and they sewed fig leaves together and made themselves coverings. And they heard the sound of the LORD God walking in the garden in the cool of the day, and Adam and his wife hid themselves from the presence of the LORD God among the trees of the garden.*
>
> Genesis 3:7-8

It was easy to blame the broker for my mess—gaining and disposing of an unseaworthy pontoon boat. We often blame others for our problems. After all, had they not tempted or enticed us into the mess, we wouldn't be in this situation! I was deceived!

> *And the LORD God said to the woman, "What is this you have done?"*
> *The woman said, "The serpent deceived me, and I ate."*
>
> Genesis 3:13

I had been enticed by the offer, the bait, a free pontoon boat. I was also deluded: The broker led me to believe that the boat was seaworthy when we talked over the phone. I was not deceived once I saw the boat. I didn't miss seeing all that rust; I plunged my head in the sand! I was admittedly stupid to put the boat on the trailer. Instead, with my head firmly in the sand, I loaded the boat and drove off.

Similarly, I was enticed by Jesse with what appeared to be a free offer, a blessing. It took longer for my eyes to open so I could see the rust. Once I pulled my head out of the sand and saw the rust—the reasons why I couldn't accept Jesse's blessing—I was a bit late and my attempt to get the boat off the trailer was not acceptable to Jesse. That was the moment I felt deluded because the blessing then suddenly felt more like a curse. As I already told you, I hoped things would change over time. As the situation got worse I had plenty of reasons to blame Jesse.

Turning to God to Flourish

I submitted to His power and allowed Him to navigate the storms of adversities pounding against the bow of my soul.

113

When storms approach you, do you hide your head in the sand? Do you blame others and make excuses for your problems or circumstances? Have you been complaining? Do you wish your circumstances would go away? It is human nature. We all spend time focusing on the impossibilities. Obviously, some of us spend more time than others dwelling on the negative aspects of adversity, trails, and tribulations. It is easy to make those sound and look much larger. I perceived such huge waves that I couldn't possibly survive. When high storms prevail you hope your anchor holds through the gale.

What could I do? My strength alone was insufficient. Eventually I asked the Lord to come and take over the helm. I wanted assurance of deliverance. I submitted to His power and allowed Him to navigate the storms of adversities pounding against the bow of my soul.

> *Thus says the LORD, who makes a way in the sea and a path through the mighty waters, who brings forth the chariot and horse, the army and the power (they shall lie down together, they shall not rise; they are extinguished, they are quenched like a wick): "do not remember the former things, nor consider the things of old. Behold, I will do a new thing, now it shall spring forth; shall you not know it? I will even make a road in the wilderness and rivers in the desert..."*
>
> Isaiah 43:16–19

I had to start focusing on the greatness of God so I could prevail and sail forward. Have you considered redirecting your energy? In other words, are you focused on the impossibility or the greatness of God? How can God use your circumstances to train you, to help you mature, to help you grow through your circumstances? Don't resist what God can use to improve you. Don't leave the place where God can help you. If you give God the helm, he will help you so you can once again flourish. Let's look at a few examples.

If you stay in the place where God can help you, you will prosper.

Consider Joseph

Recall how Joseph was stripped of his tunic and cast into a pit. Instead of killing him, his brothers took Joseph out of the pit and decided to sell him for a profit. He was purchased by Potiphar, an officer of Pharaoh. There was a blessing on the Egyptian's house for Joseph's sake (see Genesis 39: 4–5), but Joseph had another setback looming on the horizon. Potiphar's wife tried to seduce Joseph, Joseph refused, and with one of his garments in her hand, she accused Joseph of trying to lie with her (see verses 6–20). Joseph was thrown in the king's prison (see verse 20). Despite imprisonment, *"the Lord was with him; and whatever he did, the Lord made it prosper"* (Genesis 39:23). God didn't remove Joseph from prison—instead He helped Joseph gain power through his circumstances that eventually led him out of his wilderness into a position of great power (see Genesis 41:41-42). Why did Joseph thrive despite so many negative setbacks? We know that the Lord was with Joseph (see Genesis 39:2), but was there more?

Consider Palm Trees and the Garden of Eden

He pressed forward despite his circumstances and accomplished greatness. It took him many years, but he stayed the course.

Let's step ashore for a moment and see what we can learn there. It just so happens that our port is adjacent to a desert. Bob Harrison, author and seminar/conference speaker, offers a life-changing teaching audio CD series based on Psalm 92:12 called *The 7 Habits of Highly Productive Palm Trees.*

"The righteous shall flourish like a palm tree..."

Psalm 92:12

Flourish Like a Palm Tree by Mark Kuhne

Harrison researched why palm trees thrive in hostile desert environments and compared their approaches to human survival. First we should try to "avoid most desert experiences" if possible, but as we know, life happens, setbacks occur, storms of adversity surprise us, and occasionally we find ourselves in a desert (a wilderness of trials and tribulations). Like Joseph, we should "choose the correct responses to negative events." We all can agree that a fire sweeping through the land is a negative event, right? For smaller immature plants (people not well-grounded), fire can be devastating. On a mature palm tree, however, fire will burn off pests clinging to its trunk. On one hand, extremely high winds can wreak havoc. On the other hand, the palm tree is freed of older palm fronds that that are leaching water but not contributing to the tree's overall health. It is nature's way of pruning so new growth can occur sooner. Newer growth will help produce more fruit.

In other words, convert your loss to a "great spurt of growth" and bear more fruit. Obviously Harrison's multi-CD series covers much more. Discover God's plan for your life, your "purpose of flourishing," and upon leaving the desert and returning to your boat, give God the helm and let God use your circumstances along your journey to help others too. Joseph knew from his dream of greatness his reason to flourish (see Genesis 37:5–9). He pressed forward despite his circumstances and accomplished greatness. It took him many years, but he stayed the course.

Consider Adam and Eve. They walked in the Lord's presence in the garden (see Genesis 3:8). Do you think they were favored by

God? Despite their highly favored status, did God make the circumstances go away when Adam and Eve ate the fruit? Adam's and Eve's eyes were opened when they ate the fruit and felt naked, but God did not immediately hand over garments to wear: Instead, Adam and Eve "*sewed fig leaves together and made themselves coverings*" (verse 7).

When confronted by God, Adam blamed Eve and Eve blamed the serpent. The serpent was cursed by God with no hope for redemption (see Genesis 3:14, 15). After Adam and Eve were harshly rebuked and about to be sent out of the garden the "... *Lord God made tunics of skin, and clothed them*" (Genesis 3:21). The coverings made by Adam and Eve were inadequate and couldn't possibly cover their sin. Adam and Eve should have died for their sin, but God had mercy on them, killed an animal as a substitute for their redemption, and covered their sin. Today, we too are covered. God sacrificed Jesus and his blood covers our sin. I find it interesting that the serpent said nothing to God and, once it had been cursed, slithered away. Beware of people who hand something to you that seems too good to be true.

I mentioned King Nebuchadnezzar earlier when Daniel risked his life interpreting a dream with bad news. In Daniel 4:28–36, we learn that King Nebuchadnezzar's fall was due to pride: "...*Is not this great Babylon, that I have built for a royal dwelling by my mighty power and for the honor of my majesty?*" (verse 30). At that moment Daniel's interpretation of the dream was fulfilled and the king became a beast in the field. It took the king seven years in the field—a wilderness of rebellion—to learn humility, but he finally lifted his face to God and gave his heart over completely. He praised, blessed, and honored the Lord God. In other words, he turned over the helm of his "ship" to God. When he did that, his reason returned to him. The king was restored. Would you like your ship restored?

Turning from Man to God

It was like taking off my sunglasses and seeing the thunderclouds in better light—in His light.

When I gave God the helm, my perspective, my ability to reason, changed. I felt stronger. I was transformed. It was like taking off my sunglasses and seeing the thunderclouds in better light—in His light. Brian Klemmer, author and international seminar/ conference speaker, uses a two-foot-wide pair of green sunglasses and the following Scripture to illustrate transformation: *"And do not be conformed to this world, but be transformed by the renewing of your mind..."* (Romans 12:2). Klemmer teaches, *"In a revelation, something is not new, but it is new to you. Then you have had a revelation or change in how you are seeing things. The key to transformation...is having people experientially discover their sunglasses....This has to happen in an experience that emotionally effects the heart...in a real-life experience where they pierce the veil of the sunglasses."*

My situation didn't change as much as the experiences that emotionally affected my heart changed. When my heart changed, my mind changed. Can you think of a time when your perspective changed after you acknowledged the Lord your God with all your heart?

Similarly, Hezekiah did not give the Lord credit where credit was due (another form of arrogance and pride). God *"withdrew from him, in order to test him, that He might know all that was in his heart."* *"Wrath was looming"* over Hezekiah, but *"Hezekiah humbled himself for the pride of his heart"* (see 2 Chronicles 32:24–31). I cannot say for certain, but as he did with Hezekiah, maybe God was testing my heart to know all that was in my heart. I clearly didn't seek the Lord or listen to Him before making choices that led me to raging waters. And it wasn't until I was deep in those waters until I humbled myself and gave my heart and my helm fully to the Lord. Are you fully given over to the Lord? When has your faith been tested? Is your faith being tested today?

Finally, let's consider Asa, who reigned in Israel for forty-one years. In 2 Chronicles 15:2, we are told that *"...the Lord is with you while you are with Him. If you seek Him, He will be found by you...."* God is present and will defend his obedient followers. As the story unfolds, Asa and his people *"...entered into a covenant to seek the Lord God of their fathers with all their heart and with all their soul... and He was found by them, and the Lord gave them rest all around"* (2 Chronicles 15:12, 15). Later, Asa did what he thought was right and made a treaty with the king of Syria (see 2 Chronicles 16:1–12). We learn from Hanani, a seer and the Lord's prophet, that because Asa relied on the king of Syria and not God, Asa would be subject to many wars. Asa showed his lack of trust in the Lord. Asa later died from disease because *"he did not seek the Lord,"* but sought only physicians (2 Chronicles 16:12). Asa still lacked trust in the Lord and had relied only on man for a solution.

The story of Asa sounded all too familiar to me. Instead of seeking the Lord to give me understanding of my dream in which the lion was after me, I went to "man" for a solution or understanding. The Lord was speaking to me, but I didn't seek Him with all my heart and soul. I did what I thought was right and accepted a blessing, but I was later subject to a war, a battle on the high seas! I didn't show my trust in the Lord.

Unlike Asa who continued to lack trust in the Lord, eventually I gave my heart and my helm fully to the Lord. I sought the Lord and I found Him. The Lord began to give me rest. The tide changed and the Lord showed me favor in the battle.

God has seen every circumstance, I am sure He'll help you with yours—if you let Him. *"For the eyes of the Lord run to and fro throughout the whole earth, to show Himself strong on behalf of those whose heart is loyal to Him..."* (2 Chronicles 16:9). Is that great or what!? All you need for the Lord to show Himself strongly on your behalf is a heart loyal to Him! Instead of placing your trust and loyalty in man, have you given your heart and loyalty to God? Don't misunderstand me—God can work through physicians, attorneys, teachers, friends, and even enemies to help you, but your heart must seek God first. Give the Lord God the helm now! What are you waiting for?

Chapter 7

Battling the Storm

> *He who covers his sins will not prosper, but whoever confesses and forsakes them will have mercy.*
>
> Proverbs 28:13

> *Then the LORD God said, "Behold, the man has become like one of Us, to know good and evil. And now, lest he put out his hand and take also of the tree of life, and eat, and live forever"—therefore the LORD God sent him out of the garden of Eden to till the ground from which he was taken.*
>
> Genesis 3:22–23

Several calls later, I learned the junkyards would take it—for a fee. Instead I thought I could drag it out onto the ice in January, drill holes in the floats, wait for it to sink once the lake thawed in June, and charge scuba divers to come and see the wreck at forty feet deep. Well, it was just a thought. I was struggling now. How would I get rid of this? (from "The Parable of the Pontoon Boat")

I eventually figured out one reason the costs seemed so high, the consequences seemed so grave, was that my battle was also against spiritual powers that I didn't understand.

An ugly situation is costly, especially when it is your situation to solve. Our actions—choices we've made—have consequences. Overcoming consequences are not always easy. In my experience, dealing with and overcoming consequences usually takes time *and* comes at a price.

Overcoming circumstances may take blood, sweat, and tears. You may be asking, when does it all end? When will my troubles just go away? Why does this have to be so difficult? Maybe you told the Lord that your situation isn't fair! The pontoon boat was an ugly hunk of rusted steel. I couldn't hide it from my wife. I had to figure out a way to dispose of it sooner or later. As you read in my story, disposing of it hurt—literally hurt, when the steel cut my forearms. Disposing of my pontoon problem cost me blood, sweat, and money. I am not sure whether I ever cried during the process, but I cut myself several times, paid for several blades and other items, and inadvertently punched a hole in the bottom of my fishing boat.

My bigger problem with Jesse didn't cause me to lose actual blood, but there was much sweat and tears. When I finally identified my problem (lack of trust in the Lord with all my heart) and gave the helm to the Lord, the Lord favored me. Working through my circumstances became easier—not easy, just easier.

Overcoming consequences is like being in the wilderness. Remember, time in the wilderness has a purpose. A wilderness is not always a desert. It could be time on the sea at anchor while you determine your bearings, for example. It could be a situation at your workplace or a season with a very sick child or a troubled marriage in your home. No matter where your wilderness may lie, it is a place where you have an opportunity to learn and to overcome circumstances. If you overcome the circumstances, you pass the test. You move on with increased understanding, wisdom, and power. Does your battle look so big that you feel as if you are being overcome by your circumstances? Are you so deep in your wilderness that you cannot find your way out? Are you drifting about with no power? Did you lose your anchor and are at the mercy of the gale? As I said, Jesse caused me much sweat and tears. I eventually figured out one reason the costs seemed so high, the consequences seemed so grave, was that my battle was also against spiritual powers that I didn't understand.

The Spirit of Jezebel

A book, *Unmasking the Jezebel Spirit* by John Paul Jackson, helped me to understand the spiritual side of my battle against Jesse and his tactics. In chapter 6, we explored how the Jezebel spirit used deception and manipulation among three siblings. At times, I felt as though Jesse were using similar manipulative tactics against me. For the moment, let's consider Jesse to be the Jezebel spirit. I don't know if Jesse used deception to snare or entice me to accept his offer of the "blessing," but once I tried to tell him I wasn't interested, the situation changed. Jesse's tactics changed. Understanding Jezebel's tactics helped me in my responses to Jesse's repeated attacks to intimidate and manipulate me to give up and surrender to him.

Jezebel uses deception and snares to control and manipulate situations. Jezebel uses flattery, domination, intimidation, and manipulation tactics to control. Jezebel hates the uncompromising voice. Jezebel lures you in, and if luring doesn't work, she curses you for using truth and rejecting her bait. Her battle is over people. Her stronghold is stubbornness and pride, but she will be quick to point out that *you* are the stubborn one, that *you* are being selfish. She uses false power—illegitimate authority—to oppress and influence: Do it my way or you will look like a loser and there will be consequences. Selfish love feeds her agenda to seek control. Don't be surprised when Jezebel switches to self-pity to play the martyr, the victim, to manipulate.

In the Bible, Jezebel was married to King Ahab. She used Ahab to do her dirty work. Beware of statements like "We should join forces and work together." Watch out that a Jezebel spirit doesn't use a sacrificial lamb or someone else to work for him or her. In other words, you may easily spot the Jezebel spirit but not see the companion Ahab spirit. Ahab will enlist others in his cause. Ahab goes along with Jezebel when it pleases his agenda, when it complements his cause. Ahab will give up his authority. Ahab is weak and fearful. Ahab cannot make a quality decision by himself without fear. Ahab is a person called to be a leader in authority but hands it over to Jezebel. He loves position but hates confrontation. He depends on Jezebel to obtain his goals. Ahab allows the Jezebel spirit to function: His spirit nurtures Jezebel's. Keep in mind that these spirits—Jezebel and Ahab—are not isolated to one gender or the other.

Battling the Jezebel Spirit

Beware of seeking peace at the cost of truth and of relinquishing your position to her.

Confronting Jezebel with truth will cause her to consider you the enemy, as though *you* have attacked *her*. Being justified to protect herself, she counterattacks! These attacks may occur all in a day or over several months. Jezebel uses exaggeration, lies, and distortion. She will also use confusion to keep the upper hand in the battle: She will change the subject several times in the course of battle, and there is no use of logic to persuade or overcome her. Jezebel will collect information and use it against you when necessary. She may lord over you what you don't know as well as she does. She hopes that you will avoid confrontation and back down. Beware of seeking peace at the cost of truth and of relinquishing your position to her.

You must confront the Jezebel and Ahab spirits or face the inevitable later. More than once the prophet Elijah fled and hid himself from Jezebel and Ahab (see 1 Kings 17:2–4; 19:3). Fleeing and hiding are understandable and legitimate responses—at least at first. But Elijah inevitably had to confront Jezebel and Ahab (see 1 Kings 18:1–2; 21:18–19); however, he waited to do so until he was instructed by the Lord. Elijah waited upon the Lord for timing. When Elijah was in hiding, the Lord fed him super-naturally (see 1 Kings 17:4, 13–16; 19:5–8).

To help Elijah, the Lord God gave him a successor named Elisha. Elisha had Jehu anointed as king over Israel, and Jehu was given the command to strike down the house of Ahab (see 2 Kings 9:1–10). It was Jehu who asked Jezebel's own officials for help. Jezebel's officials threw her out the second-story window and Jehu drove his horses and chariots over her body, killing her (see 2 Kings 9:30–33).

During my battle with the Jezebel spirit in Jesse, someone warned me with an old saying, "You cannot beat a man at his own game." In other words, Jesse was very skilled at obligating others in his business transactions and he also used attorneys to help him obtain what he desired. I took the warning as a sign that I would be foolish to stand up against Jesse and his attorneys by myself, because I was not well-versed in those approaches.

I also "hid" at first, keeping my distance, delaying my confronta-tions with him, for example, by only returning his calls when I felt ready to do so. Once I gave the helm to the Lord, like Elijah, I also waited for the Lord to give me instructions. During my battle against Jesse, I too waited to be fed supernaturally with instructions and revelation through prayer, dreams, and any other method the Lord would use to guide me. Although the Lord did not provide me a successor, through an attorney He gave me the help I needed to confront the Jezebel spirit.

Such a spiritual battle may seem like a battle you will not win, but it will be a great relief to get rid of the Jezebel spirit. Despite what may seem like terrible consequences, fight the spirit of Jezebel (and Ahab) by desiring the things of God first. Seek the Lord with all your heart and remain righteous. By all means, do not desire the things that bring about the acceptance of other men or women. Despite how things appeared, Caleb knew that with God's help the Jews would prevail.

Then Caleb quieted the people before Moses, and said, "Let us go up at once and take possession, for we are well able to overcome it."

Numbers 13:30

But you, be strong and do not let your hands be weak, for your work shall be rewarded.

2 Chronicles 15:7

Chapter 8

The Storm Worsens

They come as broad breakers; under the ruinous storm they roll along.

Job 30:14

When your terror comes like a storm, and your destruction comes like a whirlwind, when distress and anguish come upon you.

Proverbs 1:27

Back I went to the dock to get another load. I was ready to make the next trip when Kristin asked to join me. Perhaps it looked like I was having fun. What man doesn't enjoy throwing large ragged steel chunks overboard toward a target? Are you kidding? I was finally accomplishing something. Caked in sweat and grime, I was grinning from ear to ear with steel shavings between my teeth and cuts across my hands and arms! What else could possibly happen? (from "The Parable of the Pontoon Boat")

The waters rise. The cost gets higher. When things get bad, they may get worse before they get better. By 2007, the real estate markets kept getting worse. Housing values didn't just level off—they plummeted! The predicted "housing bubble" had indeed burst. Some areas were worse off than others: Nevada was one of the bad areas. Like many people around the country, the town-home buyer of Jesse's investment couldn't get an attractive loan even if she still did want to own the townhouse. She couldn't get a loan and Jesse didn't want the townhome either. Both walked. As I had mentioned earlier, this was a common reaction: Many investors across the nation lost their deposits and didn't close on their purchase agreements.

Jesse had other real estate loses too. To help minimize his losses, he decided I should pay half of his loss on this particular town-house. He wanted me to pay up to half of the deposit that he had forfeited. His reasoning? Jesse said, "We have a LLC with both our names on it." What was he thinking? The LLC was still a shell—it wasn't funded, or capitalized, and I had never co-invested. I had been clear that this level of investing was way out of my league. How could he think I had agreed to any liability? I felt a bit like Pinocchio on Pleasure Island. The boat ride and the entry onto the island seemed effortless. The time in Las Vegas was even fun! Once on the island, though, it seemed impossible to get off. Worse, how in the world had I ended up there? What had happened?

I was frightened. A tempest rose and the waves began to spray over the gunwales. I needed a battleship, not a pontoon, if I were to survive! From my small boat, I was staring at a tidal wave. My tools, weapons, and strength alone were not enough to get me though that wave. I was afraid of the potential outcomes. I dwelled on the negative aspects of what more could go wrong. I dwelled on the possibility of losing my job or worse. My integrity could be in question and was at stake. I imagined the worst and prayed for the best. Nonetheless, I felt isolated and helpless. I didn't know who could help me.

Fighting the Jezebel Spirit in Jesse

Waves were raging and washing over the gunwales. Finally I cried out, "Lord! I am going down! Damn, I am hitting rocks...."

The water was rising all around me! Jesse would call my office or cell phone and leave a brief message, "Mark, we need to talk." After leaving his message, he would call several more times a day to see whether I would pick up the phone. At first, I "hid"—I let my phones roll over to the answering machine so I could call Jesse back when I felt ready to talk. By the end of the day or the very next morning, I would call Jesse back. Jesse would say, "Mark, you need to pay me. If you and I cannot come to terms, I'm going to have to sue you."

If he didn't level that threat at me, then he would say he was going to tell others. Tell others what?

Jesse's word. My word. Both of our names were on the LLC paperwork. What would others believe? Who would they believe? How did I get into this mess? More importantly, how was I going to get out of this mess? Early on, I had decided I wasn't even going to accept Jesse's "blessing" and here I was faced with a colossal curse and nightmare!

Do you remember how Jezebel would use information to manipulate the situation for her agenda? Jesse called me more and more. More messages were left. Again I would return his call when I was ready and hear Jesse say, "Mark, I have a document for you to sign." Jesse would say over the phone, "We can do a loan. You can make payments, low easy payments and then a balloon. You need to sign this or else…." Can you hear Jezebel making demands—"or else"?

Threatening more, Jesse called and said, "Mark, I am meeting with my collection attorney today. What are you going to do? Don't make me come after you or it will be much worse for you. Is that what you want?"

Jesse's calls continued. "Mark, time is running out. There are people who want the information I have that could be big trouble for you. Sign this agreement and I will not tell anyone…."

Later I fought the Jezebel spirit in Jesse with truth, the Word of God. I told him about Galatians 6:7, that he should not be deceived, that God will not be mocked, and that he will reap what he sows. I explained to him 1 Corinthians 6:1–9, that if he took me to court he has sided with the devil and risked losing his salvation, that believers are not to use the world's court system to solve matters against each other, and that it is "an utter failure for you that you go to law against one another." Again, he was quick to say that he had no choice. I further explained Matthew 18:25, that the Master released him of debt, but that the servant went and demanded payment from his friend. Instead of compassion and forgiveness, he demanded payment. When the Master heard of this, it didn't go well for the servant thereafter.

These calls left me physically shaking and often in tears. I had never fought this adversary before. Jezebel is a powerful foe! Fear and worry gripped my soul and grasped my throat. The enemy swooped upon me and swung a mighty sword. Wounded and weak, I often felt the cool of the valley of darkness. Alone and isolated, I wondered, "Who could help me?" I recalled Isaiah 54:17, *"No weapon formed against you shall prosper..."* and repeated it over and over. Eventually I would calm down and return to work.

Hitting the Rocks

Can you relate? Have you been on this boat facing a tempest?

My battle got worse. Jesse's calls were relentless. Through a spirit of control, manipulation, fear, and intimidation, he demanded that I agree to his terms or else. He used banking and my career to make things look extremely incriminating for me. He told me that others were after me too. He said he would take me to court and then go after much more—that I would also have to pay his attorney's expenses. The costs seemed to soar higher and higher. No matter what I said, it didn't seem to matter. He was quick to turn the conversation back to his demands and the consequences to me if I didn't succumb. He was quick to say that he had no other choice but to sue me if I didn't sign a note for a lot of money. Waves were raging and washing over the gunwales. Finally I cried out, "Lord! I am going down! Damn, I am hitting rocks. My little boat won't make it! I cannot see a lighthouse! I shouldn't even be on waters this big! What am I doing out here?! Hear me! See me! Help me! Don't let me die!"

Like a soldier at the end of a day's battle, in my sweaty, dented proverbial armor, I felt bruised, wounded, and fatigued. Weary and concerned about the next day, I stumbled home and collapsed in Kristin's arms. Within her loving arms, my head resting on her shoulder, she held me tight. I sometimes sobbed. My tears streaked the grime and blood on my face and stained her blouse. She too knew the cost of that day's battle, but held her thoughts. She too tasted the day's battle and also felt wounded. Gently setting me down, she nursed my torn flesh, replaced my bandages, and lifted my spirit.

Granted, Jesse didn't really strike with a sword, and I wasn't really bleeding, but I felt like I was. Can you relate? Next to God my Father, Kristin was strong in encouraging me to persevere and not give up. My pastors and my friends also provided the greatest encouragement, wisdom, and advice imaginable. My pastors and closest friends knew Jesse. Discreetly, I shared the details with them. They encouraged me and gave me advice. I asked other close friends for prayer support.

I have been a Bible-believing, "born-again" Christian for many years, but I cannot say I have given God the right to be my

Captain 100 percent of the time. I decided that it was time to give God the helm. "Lord, I have had all I can take; I cannot do this on my own strength. I need You to take control...NOW!"

Becoming a Shipmate

As I listened and submitted to the Lord's direction, I became stronger and confident.

When I became the shipmate and no longer the "captain," things began to change. I was led to seek help. I consulted an attorney. It was time to fight back. Jesse had been pushing me around and now he was using an attorney to intimidate me into submission. My attorney helped me understand my circumstances. He said these threats were of a desperate man. My attorney assured me that if Jesse caused me any trouble, he would defend me *pro bono*, at no charge. He explained to me why Jesse didn't have a viable case against me and explained the legal grounds for how I could fight back if necessary. He also explained that he had worked with bank regulators and how, under these circumstances, I could be defended on that front too. My actions may have been stupid, but they were not worth worrying over with respect to the law.

I didn't burst into tears, at least not right there in front of my attorney, but once I got to my car, my soul released a flood of tears. Numerous emotions from various extremes flooded every fiber within me. The Lord sent me relief. The Lord works in many ways! My battle wasn't over, but I had new weapons on deck. I was now on ship fit for battle if necessary. I also had more shipmates on deck. I had renewed courage. Not only did my attorney understand, but he also was willing to fight for me.

The storm continued. The waves began to break, however, in my favor. I could see the light—most of the time. I wasn't crashing on the rocks. I wasn't going down. Thank you, Lord.

Oddly enough, as I became more confident in where I stood and with whom I stood, the opposition seemed to sound weaker. As I listened and submitted to the Lord's direction, I became stronger and confident.

Jesse continued to call and leave messages. Then I listened to a message left by a new attorney of Jesse's: "Mr. Mark Kuhne? This is Harry Dumond, an attorney for Jesse. I understand you have an agreement and we need to talk."

I thought, "What agreement? There isn't any agreement and nothing to discuss!" When Jesse's attorney called and left me a message from his cell phone, I texted him, stating, "There is no agreement. If there is anything to discuss, call my attorney and we'll take it from there."

The Supernatural Food of Scripture

I will not only prevail, but I will be blessed when the time is right!

I pressed into many Scriptures. The Word was my weapon of truth against the Jezebel spirit: I used the Word to speak against Jesse's manipulation and intimidation. The Word was also my

136

hiding place, my refuge, where the Lord fed me supernaturally: Before returning Jesse's calls, I found a quiet place to read the Word. The Word gave me strength to battle. The Word gave me hope that I, with the Lord's help, would eventually prevail against this storm. Here are just a few examples that fed my spirit that I hope you will find nourishing too:

> *"No weapon formed against you shall prosper, and every tongue which rises against you in judgment You shall condemn. This is the heritage of the servants of the LORD, and their righteousness is from Me," says the LORD.*
>
> Isaiah 54:17

Whatever Jesse would say or threaten (his weapons and tongue), it would not work against me as long as I remained righteous in the Lord.

> *No man shall be able to stand before you all the days of your life; as I was with Moses, so I will be with you. I will not leave you nor forsake you.*
>
> Joshua 1:5

The Lord was at my side and would not forsake me.

> *He who dwells in the secret place of the Most High shall abide under the shadow of the Almighty. I will say of the LORD, "He is my refuge and my fortress; my God, in Him I will trust."*
>
> Psalm 91:1

Like Elijah, hide under the shadow of God for protection.

> *It shall come to pass in that day that his burden will be taken away from your shoulder, and his yoke from your neck, and the yoke will be destroyed because of the anointing oil.*
>
> Isaiah 10:27

In due time, the yoke of the Jezebel spirit will be broken and taken away from me because my heart, and my helm, is fully given over to the Lord.

> *So David went to Baal Perazim, and David defeated them there; and he said, "The LORD has broken through my enemies before me, like a breakthrough of water." Therefore he called the name of that place Baal Perazim.*
>
> 2 Samuel 5:20

I will break through my enemy, the Jezebel spirit. I was encouraged that my battle would be won!

> *My heart is steadfast, O God, my heart is steadfast; I will sing and give praise.*
>
> Psalm 57:7

In all things I gave the Lord praise, even when it didn't feel like I was winning. My heart and helm remained steadfast in the Lord.

I will make them and the places all around My hill a blessing; and I will cause showers to come down in their season; there shall be showers of blessing. Then the trees of the field shall yield their fruit, and the earth shall yield her increase. They shall be safe in their land; and they shall know that I am the LORD, when I have broken the bands of their yoke and delivered them from the hand of those who enslaved them. And they shall no longer be a prey for the nations, nor shall beasts of the land devour them; but they shall dwell safely, and no one shall make them afraid.

Ezekiel 34:26–28

My Hill Is a Blessing by Mark Kuhne

Again, there will be a day when I will dwell safely. I will be delivered from the Jezebel spirit that was trying to enslave me. More so, I will not only prevail, but I will be blessed when the time is right!

139

The night is far spent, the day is at hand. Therefore let us cast off the works of darkness, and let us put on the armor of light. Let us walk properly, as in the day, not in revelry and drunkenness, not in lewdness and lust, not in strife and envy. But put on the Lord Jesus Christ, and make no provision for the flesh, to fulfill its lusts.

Romans 13:12

Stay righteous in the Lord, and let Jesus fight this battle. He is now your Captain!

Blessed is the man who walks not in the counsel of the ungodly, nor stands in the path of sinners, nor sits in the seat of the scornful; but his delight is in the law of the LORD, and in His law he meditates day and night. He shall be like a tree planted by the rivers of water, that brings forth its fruit in its season, whose leaf also shall not wither; and whatever he does shall prosper.

Psalm 1:1–3

Tree Planted by Rivers of Water by Mark Kuhne

Stay in the Word. Walk righteously. Be careful who gives you counsel. In due time I will not wither, but I will bear fruit and prosper.

In obedience to John 14:13, *"And whatever you ask in My name, that I will do…"* and 1 John 5:15, *"And if we know that He hears us, whatever we ask, we know that we have the petitions that we have asked of Him,"* my wife and I wrote a petition, signed it, and filed it in our cabinet. We pleaded to the Blood of Christ over and over. We waited upon the Lord patiently wondering when we would be rescued. How bad would it get before it became better?

You realize, don't you, that there is another way? Even if you only see storm clouds gathering on the horizon, even if your boat has sprouted the tiniest of leaks—give God the helm now! Waiting to call on God to redeem, restore, and direct your path may also increase your agony and likely prolong your time in the wilderness of tribulation.

141

Don't wait for things to get extremely uncomfortable! Especially if you sense a tidal wave heading in your direction, give God the helm before the wave overcomes your boat!

Chapter 9

Am I Sinking, Lord?

Deliver me out of the mire, and let me not sink; let me be delivered from those who hate me, and out of the deep waters. Let not the floodwater overflow me, nor let the deep swallow me up; and let not the pit shut its mouth on me. Hear me, O LORD, for Your loving kindness is good; turn to me according to the multitude of Your tender mercies. And do not hide Your face from Your servant, for I am in trouble; hear me speedily. Draw near to my soul, and redeem it; deliver me...

Psalm 69:14-18

There seemed to be a little more water around our feet, but I made no mention of this. Kristin did, however. "Mark, there is water coming into the boat!" she said. (from "The Parable of the Pontoon Boat")

Why is it your wife is always right when you least want her to be?

And, does it ever work when you try to diminish the obvious?

I blew off her comment as though I knew what I was talking about. "Don't worry about it honey. All old boats take on a little water." I said. I picked up the last ragged steel sheet from the pontoon boat and heaved it overboard.

I was finally done! The old pontoon boat was no longer in our yard. It was time to rejoice! But a fountain of water was spurting up from the bottom of the boat. I had a hole in my boat! "Kristin, start bailing water while I get us back to the dock!" I ordered. I was captain of the boat, you know. Well, at least I thought I was. (from "The Parable of the Pontoon Boat")

I did have a hole in my boat, but I was not going to sink. I was (finally) giving the Lord the helm and the battle was about to tip in my favor.

Faith triumphs in trouble. That is, faith triumphs in trouble when your heart is in the right position: You are declared innocent. Righteousness is right standing with God through Jesus.

Pressed through Tribulation

Therefore, having been justified by faith, we have peace with God through our Lord Jesus Christ, through whom also we have access by faith into this grace in which we stand, and rejoice in hope of the glory of God. And not only that, but we also glory in tribulations, knowing that tribulation produces perseverance; and perseverance, character, and character, hope. Now hope does not disappoint, because the love of God has been poured out in our hearts by the Holy Spirit who was given to us.

Romans 5:1–5

In these verses in Romans, John MacArthur, editor of *The MacArthur Study Bible*, writes that *"[having been justified] underscores that justification is a one-time legal declaration with continuing results, not an ongoing process"* (page 1700). Justification has *been* done by faith. MacArthur further clarifies that *hope* in the New Testament *"contains no uncertainty; it speaks of something that is certain, but not yet realized."*

> **To overcome our tribulations, we must be willing to let God press and shape us. We must submit to our Father and let Him steer.**

Stepping off the boat for just a minute, have you ever seen a press that squeezes fluids from grapes or apples? The press contains fruit-crushing rollers. The crushing gap is adjustable. A crank raises or lowers the pressing plate (some even have rotating knives that first chop the fruit). The crank and its screw allow tremendous pressure to be ratcheted down through the plate until all the fluid is pressed out. *Tribulation* originates from words used to mean "to press," "to oppress," and "a drag used in threshing." How much pressing, how much pressure do you need to come out as sweet juice or anointed oil? It is as though God were pressing the best out of us so we can be of better use to Him. God can adjust the crushing gap because He knows just how much crushing and pressure we can bear.

The Bible also talks about pruning: "Jesus Scissorhands" will shape, cut away, or prune the limbs or ugly growths on us, so we will produce more fruit in due season (see John 15:2). He will cut away the things that hinder our walk with Him. The Holy Spirit dwells in us and will change or turn our heart (see Proverbs 21:1). As Michael Cameneti wrote in *The Missing Ingredient to Success,*

"Ultimately, the person who determines how much pruning takes place in your life is you....God will use that spoken Word to convict your heart...if you reject that conviction, the pruning will never happen and your life will still be hindered by those weights that keep you in a cycle of defeat."

Your response to the pressure and pruning also reveals your heart. As we have seen in various Bible characters noted in earlier chapters—Jezebel and Ahab; Sarai, Hagar, and Ishmael; Joseph; Asa—their responses made a huge difference in how they were used by God in His Kingdom. God promises to take care of us, to prosper us, when we listen, obey, and serve Him (see 2 Chronicles 26:5). To overcome our tribulations, we must be willing to let God press and shape us. We must submit to our Father and let Him steer. We must give God the helm!

Every branch in me that does not bear fruit He takes away; and every branch that bears fruit He prunes, that it may bear more fruit.

John 15:2

Before I tell you the end of my story with Jesse, let's return to a point in the battle that took endurance to persevere through the tribulation or tempest. My endurance or strength came when I handed the helm over to the Lord. For example, the Lord gave me instructions or tactics to follow through a particular dream.

My Fight with a Demon

In September 2007, just when I thought the worst was going to happen, the Lord provided another dream to guide me and encourage me in this fight against *"principalities, against powers, against the rulers of the darkness of this age, against spiritual hosts of wickedness in the heavenly places"* (Ephesians 6:12).

I was in a brightly lit operating room. The rather large, rectangular room held several operating tables parallel to each other, but not so close that the other tables had any bearing to me. I was the only person present.

Apparently I was dressed as a doctor, a surgeon, because I held a scalpel. Instead of standing on the floor next to the table, though, I was standing on the table. I was standing at the feet of a body that was lying on the table. On the other end of the table standing and facing me was a demonic spirit that appeared as a faceless man and represented the body on the operating table. The body on the table was Jesse! This demonic spirit stood at the "head" of the Jesse on the table.

The fight that was about to ensue was not against Jesse (flesh and blood) but against dark powers: a demon. The demon had bare arms and extended his arm, taunting me, "Go ahead, cut me!" Figuring it was a trap if I got too close to the demon's grasp, I tried to slash, but I kept my distance, staying at my end of the table. As his taunting intensified, I purposely buried the scalpel deep into the demon's wrist. Then I dragged the scalpel across the wrist and out. Again, I made sure that I kept my distance. I didn't want to be grabbed or have the scalpel taken from me and used against me. Having field-dressed several deer in my life I know how a sharp knife works through hide or skin, thick or thin. The scalpel should have cut easily through that wrist—but it didn't. I struggled to drag the scalpel through—this demon's skin was woody or fibrous.

I made several deep cuts across the demon's arms and wrists. The demon looked like a regular man, but no blood came out. Blood, however, surrounded me. I glanced over my right shoulder. There against the wall was Christ nailed to the cross. Blood was splattered everywhere. My first thought was my sins nailed Christ on that cross. Secondly, I realized His blood protected me. The presence of Christ kept the demon at bay while I sliced the demon's arms and tried to kill him.

Suddenly the scene changed. I had jumped down and I ran away from the operating table. In pursuit, the demon ran after me. I ran down an aisle like one in a department store or grocery store with boxes on the shelves. As I ran, I pulled boxes off the shelves and created obstacles that slowed the demon's pursuit. I reached the end of the aisle, turned around, and shot the demon. One shot and the demon was gone! Yet I do not remember having a gun in my hand. I cannot remember seeing the demon die, hit the ground, or disappear, but it definitely was no longer a threat or in my presence.

One could draw much from this dream: It is rich with imagery and symbolism to interpret. Suffice it to say, the body on the table was Jesse threatening me. Again, my fight was not against his flesh but against the spirit of darkness. Jesus was there to protect me. The dream instructed me to delay Jesse in his pursuit of my cooperation with his agenda. In the dream I ran and threw boxes in the aisle to slow the demon. With Jesse, I didn't answer my phone immediately, carefully timed my returned calls to him, and answered some of his threats with Bible verses "to slow him down" with the Word. I also refused to meet or cooperate with his timing.

No Longer Sinking

The spirit of fear and worry approached, but I did not let the spirit stay on my boat.

Time did pass. Calls from Jesse would sometimes stop for a few months. I would begin to think the battle was over and Jesse had given up. Then out of the blue, he would call as though only a couple of days had passed. Again Jesse would demand, "Sign an agreement, a promissory note, or else I will sue, and others will come after you." It was the same story and demand every time. As time passed, however, my "delay" seemed to be working. I noticed that I felt more in control of my feelings. I was not quite as shaken as I had been earlier. There were times, however, that I thought it would be a relief to end this madness, surrender, and sign a note, to just be done with it. The spirit of fear and worry approached, but I did not let the spirit stay on my boat.

My pastor and my wife Kristin both felt in their spirits to tell me to "delay." Their words confirmed the message of my "operating room" dream to create obstacles and delay until the right time. As some Bible verses suggest, there were seasons for everything.

The Lord has His right timing and since I gave Him the helm I didn't wish to step out of sync with His timing. When Jesse had an attorney call me, when I heard the saying about beating a man at his own game, I felt it was time. It was time for me to also seek the advice of an attorney. I wasn't going to press any charges or initiate any legal action. I just wanted to know what I was up against in case his threats materialized. The attorney's advice gave me more reason to stand my ground: Neither Jesse with his threats nor others "coming after me" would have much of a case.

So how did my battle with Jesse end? I had received the message from a new attorney representing Jesse. I had texted Mr. Dumond, in short, telling him to call my attorney. I told my attorney to expect the call from Mr. Dumond, and Mr. Dumond did call. My attorney asked him for copies of the evidence that he and Jesse seemed to have against me. My attorney called me back and said, "Mark, Mr. Dumond called, but I doubt they will send me anything to review. We'll see what happens. Chances are this will just go away."

Since then, I have yet to hear anything more. Will Jesse sail on my seas and attempt to overtake me and my boat again? I don't know. I prefer that he navigate different seas and stay away from me. In prayer, I forgave him and wished him well on his journey.

I doubt I will restore my relationship with Jesse. Forgiveness is not the same as restoration. To restore, a person you must trust another again. When Jesse threatened to destroy my life, I found it difficult to think I could ever again trust him. Does the fear of this man coming after me still haunt me? I have thoughts now and then, but I don't let those thoughts take hold at the helm of my boat. Those thoughts are more like waves that act up but settle down fairly quickly. Who knows when the next encounter will occur? I do know that the Lord is in control and that no weapon formed against me will prosper.

No, I am not sinking. For a moment, there may be a hole and some water in my boat. I may shake or tremble in the presence of a demon, but my Lord will rescue me and not forsake me. My ship will sail. Jesse wasn't my worst enemy in this battle; the spirit of Jezebel was. I was also my own enemy when I allowed my trust in a person to cloud my ability to discern. The Lord my God has the helm now! The Bible says to *"...submit to God. Resist the devil and he will flee from you. Draw near to God and He will draw near to you. Cleanse your hands, you sinners; and purify your hearts, you double-minded...Humble yourselves in the sight of the Lord, and He will lift you up"* (James 4:7–8, 10). I will not sink in the *"day of adversity"* (see Proverbs 24:10). I will remain righteous—Christ-like) I will be strong and endure. I will not quit. Victory is mine—and God's.

And what about you—is there a raging sea in front of you waiting to pull you in? *"A prudent man foresees evil and hides himself..."* (Proverbs 22:3). Are the waters rising? Find a safe haven and get out of the way. By now I hope you can recognize trouble on the horizon and be prepared before the storm hits. Storms will hit. The devil will return when opportunities arise.

> *Now when the devil had ended every temptation, he departed from Him until an opportune time.*
>
> Luke 4:13

Just as Jesse's "I want to bless you" knocked on my door, and similar to the Potiphar's wife's sexual advances knocking proverbially on Joseph's door, we can see that sin will seek you out. Are you prepared with weapons that work? Do you wear the full armor of God? As you read about my weaknesses, perhaps you recognized some of your own. Just remember, if you give God the helm—and serve as a worthy crewmember—you overcome any rough seas of adversity and have victory though your circumstances!

> *Let us run with endurance the race that is set before us.*
>
> Hebrews 12:1

Chapter 10

Assessing Damage from the Storm

> For the wages of sin is death, but the gift of God is eternal life in Christ Jesus our Lord.
>
> Romans 6:23

Kristin and I made it back. With her bailing water and my quick reaction to head back to shore, we survived with only wet feet. We pulled the boat onto the shore and I stared at the hole in my fishing boat. By now I was thinking the free pontoon boat I had hauled, dismantled, and sunk, had become more expensive than a new twenty-four-foot aluminum pontoon boat with a 50-horsepower motor, bimini top, and a load of extras.

Why didn't I just say "No, thanks," when I first saw the rusty boat? On second thought, that broker didn't really help me with deals that much. Why had I been sooooo stupid? One boat sunk—and another boat that almost sank and now needed repair. At this point I could not even afford to think about how "free" that old pontoon boat was. (from "The Parable of the Pontoon Boat")

To the extent possible, if you learn from others' trials and tribulations, you receive a free ride to understanding and wisdom.

To overcome is to conquer or subdue your circumstances, obstacles, and adversities. In overcoming my tribulations of the pontoon boat and townhome investment, let me share with you what I paid in terms of mental anguish and personal integrity. I may not be able to add up the actual cost that I paid to dispose of that free pontoon boat. As I told you already, it was by no means free. With respect to my battle with Jesse, I didn't die, but I must know and remember the cost as a reminder to never sail that sea again! That battle was extremely painful in many ways. Pain or the threat of pain can be a tremendous motivator. Do you remember Klemmer's key to transformation through an experience that emotionally affects the heart? My real-life experience pierced the veil of my perception when I gave God the helm. Although the devil may tempt me to travel that sea in the future, I have no desire to experience that tribulation or trial ever again, and I will be better prepared to stand up against that devil and find safer waters for me and my boat.

So what did it cost? The education was priceless. I cannot fathom the hours I spent studying. Although books I read helped me along the way—the Bible being the greatest help of all—the lessons learned didn't come by way of college or university classes. The lessons came by experience. Benjamin Franklin (*Poor Richard's Almanac*, November 1743) said, "*Experience keeps a dear school, yet fools learn in no other.*" I have no argument with his statement. I would only add that experience comes at a great price when it is yours to pay. To the extent possible, if you learn from others' trials and tribulations, you receive a free ride to understanding and wisdom. In any event, your learning curve should be shorter and less expensive.

What I paid in actual currency paled in comparison to the things that were not paid in cash. They included lost opportunities, shame, guilt, integrity, mental anguish, health, and more. Based on my perceptions, I made some of those issues more costly than they needed to be. Nonetheless, they were real to me.

As one example, during the Jesse tribulation, I received an attractive job offer that came with a much higher salary. I accepted the offer but in the final consideration my integrity was an issue… that clouded their ability to trust me. Under the circumstances, I withdrew my acceptance and the potential employer concurred. I became afraid that this "integrity question," like an octopus in the sea of opportunities, had tentacles that could reach out and cause me issues elsewhere. I passed on similar opportunities offered to me by headhunters because I feared that octopus. I didn't even bother to interview.

Shame and guilt are interesting creatures: They can be self-imposed. Much of the shame and guilt I felt were just that—self-imposed internal feelings that were based on what others might think, know, or choose to think. Remember, I questioned how someone would perceive my actions. I questioned who they

155

would believe or what they would believe. The lost job opportunity fed my shame and guilt. What would happen to my reputation? What if it affected my current position? What if I lost my career? I questioned my worth. Shame and guilt, as well as uncertainty, grew at tremendous rates until I handed the helm to God. Based on the Word, I had to trust in Him, trust that regardless of the potential outcomes, He would place me exactly where I needed to be and He would protect me.

In prayer, I begged the Lord to purify my heart. I wanted to feel clean again. All I have to say is to be careful what you ask for because you just might get it! Remember that wine press that cuts, crushes, and presses the grapes until sweet juice is obtained? Remember when I said I felt as though I had been pruned by "Jesus Scissorhands"? Our church congregation has an annual world mission conference that invites apostles (our church supports) to visit from various countries. My wife and I attended the smaller meetings over the two to three days prior to the conference. In those meetings, we each would recap our year. In the meeting after the onset of the battle with Jesse, I tried to describe my mental anguish of feeling attacked and oppressed by the enemy. I equated it to being in combat. Like a soldier, I felt cut, battered, bloody, and bruised. Many nights I was exhausted and wept in my wife's arms. The following year I told the group I had been pruned by "Jesus Scissorhands." At least when Jesus prunes, He cuts to help you flourish, grow, and bear more fruit. Jezebel, on the other hand, cuts to steal, kill, and destroy!

As one may guess, adversity can cause stress that affects one's health negatively. As I perceived my adversities to be growing, the stress grew too. When my phones rang, I would have anxiety attacks. When I saw unknown numbers appear on my cell phone, my heart rate increased. When I saw Jesse's number, my heart absolutely raced. I felt sick to my stomach listening to his messages. Avoiding his calls until I felt better prepared to answer him took its toll. His calls also interrupted my ability to think clearly at work: Preparing to respond to him would often consume me.

After conversing with Jesse, I felt mentally and physically drained. By night I wanted to collapse, but I had a family to care for and they needed a husband and father. I often crawled into bed early but usually woke throughout the night with more questions and uncertainty bearing down on me— questions like, "Will I succumb to depression and drug therapy? Will I have a mental breakdown and be hospitalized? Will my heart physically give out? How much more can I handle?"

At one point I was about to sink: My little boat was not prepared to face a tidal wave. I wanted to turn my boat around and run, but I knew I couldn't outrun that tidal wave. I had to face this wave to overcome and conquer my fears. Kristin, my pastors, and close friends were usually there to throw me a personal floatation device (PFD), but I needed more than a PFD to survive. I needed the supernatural strength of the Lord. I needed Him as captain of my boat. Once I gave God the helm, the tide changed, and the turbulent waters subsided!

Is the Lord your Captain? Have you plotted a course together that will steer your boat around as many storms as possible?

How are you growing spiritually?

Chapter 11

Steady as You Go!

> *For though by this time you ought to be teachers, you need someone to teach you again the first principles of the oracles of God; and you have come to need milk and not solid food. For everyone who partakes only of milk is unskilled in the word of righteousness, for he is a babe. But solid food belongs to those who are of full age, that is, those who by reason of use have their senses exercised to discern both good and evil.*
>
> Hebrews 5:12–14

Surely by now you can see what it cost me to insist on captaining my boat by myself through rough seas. And I hope in addition to recognizing some of your own stubborn steering habits, you're beginning to see the advantages of turning the helm over to God. So what specifically can you can do to give Him the helm, to overcome the storms in your life? How do you become spiritually mature (*"of full age"*) to *"discern both good and evil"*?

How do you become spiritually mature (*"of full age"*) to *"discern both good and evil"*?

Negative versus Positive Routines

Recently I read "Sales Leadership in Turbulent Times," an article by Ned Miller in an MZ Bierly publication. As I read, I kept seeing applications to overcome not only turbulent circumstances in sales or business but any difficult circumstances. Really, what is the difference?

Miller stated that *"rituals are routines."* They may pull at you to knock you off track. Think about it, the world system pulls at you. If you doubt the power of that pull (or push), I suggest you read Malcolm Gladwell's books, *The Tipping Point* and *Blink.* We are highly programmed: We think, act, and respond certain ways that are triggered by a variety of things. Often we are triggered subconsciously—we don't even realize it!

Miller's article did acknowledge that rituals can also serve as a positive framework. Overcoming circumstances requires discipline and takes a conscious effort. Instead of drifting on (negative) rituals that do not work in our favor, we need to design positive rituals to drive desired changes that do work in our favor. Doing the same things and expecting different results is ludicrous!

Moses, at the hand of God, led the Jews into the wilderness of transition. They copped an attitude and ended up in the wilderness of rebellion for forty years! God understands human nature. To help His people, God gave Moses numerous laws, or positive rituals, to help keep the Jews focused and moving in a desirable direction.

Miller went on to explain, *"Without rituals, people often lose focus and honest attempts to change behavior fizzle."* God already said this in Proverbs 29:18: *"Where there is no revelation, the people cast off restraint..."* In other words, where there is no focus on the Word, the people rebel and eventually perish. You need to have a godly vision, a purpose. Are you making decisions driven by godly purpose about where to spend your time, talents, and treasure? What is pulling or pushing you off the path that God designed for you? Do you find yourself reacting to forces of the world?

Miller further explains, *"...when the will is there but the discipline isn't, new rituals provide a framework in which breakthroughs often take place. Rituals enable us to structure our lives in the face of competing demands."* Competing demands can be turbulent circumstances. Are circumstances dragging you down? Worse, is your spirit broken and have you lost hope? Perhaps you are waiting for your breakthroughs and nothing seems to happen. Create new rituals to restructure your life so you can overcome and take advantage of your circumstances.

12 Ways to Walk in Christ

Overcoming circumstances and strongholds is rarely easy. Circumstances or strongholds can be spiritual, not just natural, so trying to overcome them by natural means may not work. What works best is to gain victory through your walk in Christ. Miller suggests developing new routines to help you create *"new behaviors that can become automatic and relatively painless."* We can apply Miller's suggestion to better focus on the Lord. The better you are at designing new rituals that help you grow spiritually and please the Lord, the more quickly you will break through to a new level of maturity, power and authority. Seek ways to please the Lord in all you do so the windows of Heaven will be opened for you. The Lord opens the windows of Heaven to favor and bless you so you can help edify the Kingdom of God! In other words, rewards come when you walk in His way.

> *"If they obey and serve Him, they shall spend their days in prosperity, and their years in pleasures. But if they do not obey, they shall perish by the sword, and they shall die without knowledge."*
>
> Job 36:11–12

To walk in His way, you can take many steps to create a framework or positive routines or rituals to overcome and take advantage of your circumstances sooner than later. The more of these you build into your routines, the stronger you will be, and the better equipped you will be at overcoming. Remember as you move forward to use the right motives to please God. Submit yourself to God and His Word (see James 4:10). God will lift you up!

1. Fear God, Submit to His Authority, and Give Him the Helm
2. Fix What You Can—Review, Repair, Repent
3. Honor the Lord Your God

4. Pray and Fast

5. Study, Read Your Bible Daily, and Live to Learn

6. Discover Your Calling

7. Press In

8. Journal and Immerse Yourself

9. Disciple and Edify Others

10. Seek Counsel

11. Plan from Kingdom Principles

12. Practice Patience

1. Fear God, Submit to His Authority, and Give Him the Helm

First and most importantly, fear God, submit to His authority, and give Him the helm. What specifically can you do to give him the helm? Practicing the twelve methods on this list is a good start.

2. Fix What You Can—Review, Repair, Repent

• **Review.** Part of maturing and overcoming your circumstances is to review and recognize the part you played in creating your problems. This is the time to search your soul and ask yourself many questions. What did I do and what can I do in the future to avoid a similar situation so I am not in need of overcoming these circumstances again? For example, I have learned that my biggest weakness causing me problems was my gullibility when I highly trusted someone and ignored the need for discernment. So in the future, I need to give the helm to God, assess the situation and wait for His instruction (including others to provide counsel and wisdom) especially when outside my area of expertise, before departing from port, so I can avoid as many storms of adversity as possible.

• **Repair.** To the extent possible, do what you can to repair the situation. Certainly, some things you personally cannot fix. Apologies work in most circumstances but sometimes offend in others. Seek the Lord for guidance on how to proceed. If nothing else, at least honor the involved or harmed parties in your prayers.

• **Repent.** Get your heart right with God. The truth about sin is that you can deny it, rationalize or justify it, or turn away from it. Stop the behavior, repent, forgive others, ask God for forgiveness, receive that forgiveness, and move on. If you do not move on, guilt will overcome you and keep you from walking ahead in your calling. After repenting, walk in obedience.

If we confess our sins, He is faithful and just to forgive us our sins and to cleanse us from all unrighteousness. If we say that we have not sinned, we make Him a liar, and His word is not in us.

1 John 1:9–10

3. Honor the Lord Your God

• **Worship**. Worship on Sundays, of course, but do you worship the Lord in small frequent doses—while in your shower, car, or boat, for instance? Frequent worship keeps your eyes on

Christ. Worship shows your love for the Lord. Our Father in heaven wants us to love and revere Him. Corporate worship is a joint effort: In better churches there are spiritual and natural support available. In our church, for example, we have a gold line that runs the length of the alter area. Our services usually end with numerous people at the gold line for prayer support. Worship goes hand in hand with praise.

• **Praise**. If you are a sorry sap wallowing in a pity party, worrying about your circumstances, do you think the Holy Spirit really wants to dwell in you? Where do you like to hang out? I would venture to say that given a choice, you would avoid a group of negative people. Worry can lead to fear. Fear will cripple you and steal your joy. Do you think the devil graciously gave you a pretty package of circumstances so you could bask in joy? No. Keep your eyes on Christ and praise the Lord!

According to Psalm 148:1-4, and using the seven Hebrew words for *praise*, here are seven ways to praise the Lord:

> *Praise the Lord!*
> *HALLAL the Lord from the heavens;*
> *YADAH Him in the heights!*
> *BARAF Him, all His angels;*
> *TEHILLAH Him, all His hosts!*
> *ZAMAR Him, sun and moon;*
> *TODAH Him, all you stars of light!*
> *SHABACH Him, you heavens of heavens,*

And you waters above the heavens! (Psalm 148:1–4, author emphasis)

- **Hallal** is to make a show or rave about, to glory in or boast upon, to be clamorously foolish about your adoration of God.
- **Yadah** is to hold out or lift the hand, to revere or worship with extended hands, thankfulness, and thanksgiving.
- **Baraf** is to bless, kneel, and salute, to show respect and recognition to a superior by assuming a prescribed position.
- **Tehillah** is to sing Hallal, a new song, a hymn of spontaneous praise glorying God in song.
- **Zamar** is to touch the strings or parts of a musical instrument, to play upon it, to make music, accompanied by the voice, to celebrate in song and music, give praise, sing forth praises and psalms.
- **Todah** is an extension of the hand, adoration, a choir of worshipers, confession, sacrifice of praise, thanksgiving.
- **Shabach** is to address in a loud tone, a loud adoration, a shout, proclaiming with a loud voice unashamed, to glory, triumph, a testimony of praise.

Praise the Lord! by Mark Kuhne

Be *anxious for nothing, but in everything by prayer and supplication, with thanksgiving, let your requests be made known to God; and the peace of God, which surpasses all understanding, will guard your hearts and minds through Christ Jesus.*

Philippians 4:6–7

4. Pray and Fast

• **Pray more than ever and then some.** Tell Him the desires of your heart. Tell Him that you want your heart to harmonize with His will for you. Ask God lots of questions and actually wait for His answers. Schedule and block out prayer time *with* the Lord. Personally, I spend the beginning of every day with the Lord and then integrate prayer into everything I do throughout the day. I accept this as critical to my success. It is nonnegotiable. Converse with the Lord as though He were visibly sitting next to you as your closest advisor and confidant—He is all that, so you might as well start talking to Him! At the risk of my wife Kristin saying that I need to talk more when we drive together, don't you get a little uncomfortable when you are in a car with someone who never talks to you? Talk to God.

- **Fast.** I gave up pounding the snooze button on my alarm clock in the morning and decided to spend that extra time reading my Bible, praying, and journaling. Lord knows I could also stand to give up a few meals and fast food too. But dieting is not the purpose of fasting, even if I do need to lose a few pounds.

Delight yourself also in the LORD, and He shall give you the desires of your heart.

Psalm 37:4

5. Study, Read Your Bible Daily, and Live to Learn

- **Take classes.** Don't be spiritually immature (see Hebrews 3:12-14). Let's face it, we do not know as much as we should. We can improve our lives and the lives of others by expanding our knowledge and understanding. Our church has weekly classes and we attend those regularly. What classes are you currently taking? Where are you spending your time? Less time in front of the television and similar worldly teachers (at bars, enjoying ungodly movies and activities, surfing the Internet, etc.) and more time in Bible classes will make you better prepared to overcome your circumstances.

- **Attend and host seminars.** We have attended Bob Harrison's Increase Events in Hawaii and Florida: These are three- to five-day day seminars on steroids. In addition to the great teaching from Bob Harrison, his speakers—too many to name here—are phenomenal and give you tools to build your boat into a ship. You'll learn to think bigger. His Increase Events are designed to help you take your boat to deeper waters. We were so impressed that Kristin and I created a "mini-event" in Minneapolis and invited Bob Harrison and Brian Klemmer to speak. Since then Harrison has preached at our church on several occasions and we have hosted a Klemmer "Champions' Workshop" and "Personal Mastery" seminar. We also hosted an event with John Bevere as our primary speaker.

- **Read your Bible every day and meditate on His Word.** The Bible is the ultimate book—it is His Word! To go deeper than ever with your relationship with God, you must spend time with Him and His Word. Let God be your Captain: He'll guide you so you are not deceived and so you know where to walk in obedience to His Word. *"And Jesus answered and said to them: 'Take heed that no one deceives you'"* (Matthew 24:4). You can test all things according to the Word. This is the rulebook for discernment. Learn the Word to change your heart. Then hear with your heart the Holy Spirit within you.

- **Use meditative CDs or DVDs.** Joshua 1:8: tells us that *"This Book of the Law shall not depart from your mouth, but you shall meditate in it day and night, that you may observe to do according to all that is written in it. For then you will make your way prosperous, and then you will have good success."* Kristin and I have started creating DVDs to help people with godly meditation called "contemplative prayer."

The first DVD is "Tree of Life, A Contemplative Prayer." It is based on my painting *"Tree of Life."* Kristin teaches for the first twelve minutes and I guide the listener through mediation and contemplation using the image of the painting for about thirty minutes. You will find this book, our DVDs, and more at www. OvercomingForLife.com.

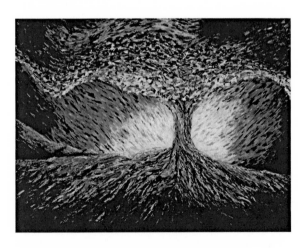

Tree of Life by Mark Kuhne

Steady as You Go!

- **Read books**. They expand your knowledge, understanding, and wisdom. Hey, reading this book counts! Check the Additional Resources I provide on pages 208–212 for other books to read. Read to prepare yourself. Become educated about new routines that can help overcome your circumstances. Prepare in advance for new circumstances.

6. Discover Your Calling

Discover, practice, and become an expert in the area God wants you to be an expert. Ask the Holy Spirit to reveal your calling to you. Don't fight what you are called to do. Doing what the Lord calls you to do brings fulfillment and joy. This is where you are anointed and blessed by God.

Mike Francen of Francen World Outreach said in his book, *Destiny*, *"The greatest building has yet to be erected. The greatest invention yet to be patented. The greatest song has yet to be composed, the greatest book yet to be written. The most profound thought has yet to be perceived, the most amazing theory yet to be proven. The most beautiful poem has yet to be penned, the most powerful sermon yet to be preached. The grandest victory has yet to be realized. The greatest wealth has yet to be accumulated. The largest offering yet to be given. The greatest day has yet to dawn."* Not everything is done yet. There is much more to do and accomplish. You alone are uniquely qualified to edify the kingdom of God. What have you done with your giftedness? What are you going to do? More importantly, what has God called you to do?

- **Follow your passion.** What were some of your childhood dreams? I once dreamed of being an artist but gave it up because my father said I couldn't make any money at it. Maybe my father was right, but it was still a dream, a passion, for me to explore. Instead, I quit painting. In late 2007 the Lord touched me and said, "Paint!" So I am painting again. Time will tell whether I make any money at it. My greatest painting has yet to be painted!

- **Learn about who you are.** Do you know who you truly are? There are various books and tools to help you understand yourself better. I used Eddie Rasnake's *Using Your Spiritual Gifts* to help me understand my giftedness. I also used Tom Rath's book and related Internet tool *Strengths Finder 2.0* to help uncover my top talents. I took the Step II version of the Myers-Briggs Type Indicator (MBTI) as part of a personality inventory exercise at work. We also took the Kolbe A Index to measure our "instinctive method of operation (MO)" that also identified the ways I would be most productive. By far the most fun online assessment was "The Flag Page" that measures one thing—passion—as part of a video marriage seminar by Mark Gungor that our church hosted.

Now an angel of the Lord spoke to Philip, saying, "Arise and go..."

Acts 8:26

The point is, do various things to understand and improve yourself. Involve the Holy Spirit to reveal assignments and divine connections (right place, right time). Assignments require preparation, and expect the Lord's favor and even the miraculous to help you along. Your work should be something that gives you satisfaction. When your work satisfies you, you are blessed and you are a blessing to others. It is more than just a job. You feel good about what you are doing. You are serving others in a way that also brings you joy.

7. Press In

Whatever you do, do not quit. Move forward as best you can and do not quit. Some days will seem to get the best of you, but do not give the enemy your helm—give the helm to God instead. Rest at anchor, mend your wounds, and get back in the boat moving toward your destination. If the Lord has your helm, if you honor Him, *"…He will set you high above all nations…"* (Deuteronomy 26:19) and the yoke upon you will be broken (see Ezekiel 34:26–27).

You are in good company. Jesus was in the desert with Satan in the wilderness of testing and trials. Power and authority, and the wisdom to use them, grow from experiences. But it was not power or authority that Jesus used in this wilderness to overcome temptation. It was an understanding of the Word of God: He spoke the Word and, through the Word, He had the power and authority of God. Know that temptation and evil may depart for a season, but also know it will return at an opportune time (see Luke 4:1).

When Rev. Chris D'Amico spoke at our church he told us, *"You must play to win. You must press on to bigger victories. Just don't give up. Fear is the darkroom where your negatives are developed."*

> *But you, be strong and do not let your hands be weak, for your work shall be rewarded!*
>
> 2 Chronicles 15:7

You don't have to sail on every rough wave—find a better route. Some seas are best avoided. When you are facing a tidal wave, batten down the hatches and let God point your boat in the right direction.

> *Not that I have already attained, or am already perfected; but I press on, that I may lay hold of that for which Christ Jesus has also laid hold of me.*
>
> Philippians 3:12

8. Journal and Immerse Yourself

• **Journal**. Journals and other writing tools can guide you through Biblical topics and issues. I started with a *Driven by Eternity Devotional Workbook* by John Bevere and then went to blank paper to chart my course as the Holy Spirit led me. I basically journaled one chapter of Psalms each day and then moved to other books as the Lord led me. I wrote several of my prayers in my journal fully expecting the Lord to answer me sooner or later. He did! If Moses advised kings in Deuteronomy to write a copy of the law (the "Word") in a book and to read it all the days of their life, that they may learn to revere the Lord and obey the Word, and that it would prolong their days (see Deuteronomy 17:18–20), then I think it would be wise for us to read our Bible every day and write in a journal about what we learned in the Bible. What was good enough for kings is good enough for me.

• **Immerse yourself in affirmations, music, books, DVDs, teaching CDs, and such.** Enough cannot be said about writing down affirmations and repeating them regularly. Without any effort at all, you already affirm many negative thoughts throughout your entire day and night. You might as well give positive affirmations some chance of seeding your mind, soul, and spirit. Before you know it, those seeds grow. God does the watering. Don't dwell on your circumstances. Eliminate negative speech. Repeat out loud positive speech daily. Someone once said, *"Your mouth is the rudder that guides your boat; use it properly."* The Lord *spoke* everything into existence. What are you speaking into your existence?

You are worthy. You are His royal heir, His child. Not only ask, but believe and receive what your Father in Heaven wishes to give you. Did you hear that? Say it out loud! Startle your spouse and everyone sitting around you. Boldly declare, "I am worthy! I am a child of God! I believe and receive what my Father in Heaven gives me!" Call out what you believe and will receive: checks, supernatural promises, breakthrough, miracles, benefits, sales, commissions, favorable settlements, income, release of gifts, anointing to destroy your debt, and reduced expenses so you can better serve Christ and promote His Gospel. There is power in your tongue. My changes did not occur overnight, but I didn't give up. When I reach one destination, I chart a course for the next one. I daily keep my aim on my targeted destination.

Death and life are in the power of the tongue, and those who love it will eat its fruit.

Proverbs 18:21

Finally, brethren, whatever things are true, whatever things are noble, whatever things are just, whatever things are pure, whatever things are lovely, whatever things are of good report, if there is any virtue and if there is anything praiseworthy—meditate on these things. The things which you learned and received and heard and saw in me, these do, and the God of peace will be with you.

Philippians 4:8–9

I can do all things through Christ who strengthens me.

Philippians 4:13

9. Disciple and Edify Others

• **Edify and serve others**. Serving others also serves the Lord. You help edify or build up the kingdom of God. Help others succeed, even when you are going through your tough times. When I helped others, God helped me grow through my circumstances. Learn to do things for others besides your immediate family. Deuteronomy 17:16–17 says, *"But he shall not multiply horses for himself...nor shall he greatly multiply silver and gold for himself."*

> *Let us therefore come boldly to the throne of grace, that we may obtain mercy and find grace to help in time of need.*
>
> Hebrews 4:16

Just as we can go boldly to the throne of God to obtain mercy and help in time of our need, we are called to be like Christ and help others too.

• **Go on mission trip(s)**. To go *"...make disciples of all nations..."* is the great commission (Matthew 28:19-20). If you want to open your eyes and awake the spirit within you, attend an open-stage crusade in a third- or fourth-world country! No doubt, you will witness the power of the Holy Spirit bring multitudes to the Lord and use healings as signs, wonders, and miracles! You will never be the same, ever! Once you know that you know that you know that our Lord is a living and powerful God and you see with your own eyes their healings and hear with your own ears their testimonies, you will be hooked for life.

- **Teach.** Nothing grounds you more in what you know than when you teach what you know to someone else.

> *And the things that you have heard from me among many witnesses, commit these to faithful men who will be able to teach others also.*
>
> 2 Timothy 2:2

- **Create or join a small group.** If you share similar circumstances, beware of creating a pity party! Use this book or others to guide your discussions. The Lord calls us to encourage one another (see Hebrews 3:13), to comfort each other (see 1 Thessalonians 5:11), to build each other up, and to comfort together (see 2 Corinthians 1:4). A small group can help keep members on a righteous path. A small group is an excellent place to receive encouragement that helps people overcome their circumstances.

> *Beware, brethren, lest there be in any of you an evil heart of unbelief in departing from the living God; but exhort one another daily, while it is called "Today," lest any of you be hardened through the deceitfulness of sin.*
>
> Hebrews 3:12–13

Blessed be the God and Father of our Lord Jesus Christ, the Father of mercies and God of all comfort, who comforts us in all our tribulation, that we may be able to comfort those who are in any trouble, with the comfort with which we ourselves are comforted by God.

2 Corinthians 1:3–4

10. Seek Counsel

The ultimate Counselor is the Holy Spirit. He was sent here to dwell in us. Tap into His power. By waiting and listening after I prayed—sometimes for many minutes—I learned to hear His voice. Other times he speaks to me through dreams and visions—I have already shared several of those with you.

Include other godly people: Get support or coaching from those who have overcome similar circumstances. Be careful, however, when receiving directive advice from those who are not spiritually mature or qualified. For bigger decisions, take the advice you received to others to get second and third opinions.

Know what you are getting into. Do not be gullible. Now when I make a significant arrangement with someone, I require something on paper. No paper, no deal! Don't get so wrapped up thinking about the upside and neglect the downside and potential costs if your arrangement doesn't work out. Define the upside and the downside on paper. Even if you do not use a signed agreement, write out the positive and negative aspects.

Sometimes on less important arrangements I send the party an e-mail that recaps our conversation or arrangement and asks for their confirmation. On something much bigger or more complicated, I recommend using an attorney to guide you. Remember the e-mail exchange between the siblings over a debt? Jeremiah wanted to consider an attorney if they created a debt "arrangement" between them and their father.

> *For by wise counsel you will wage your own war, and in a multitude of counselors there is safety.*
>
> Proverbs 24:6

11. Plan from Kingdom Principles

Today I try to make plans using biblical principles. For example, to avoid selfishness, I want all involved or affected by my plans to benefit. I like Napoleon Hill's statement in his book *Think & Grow Rich*: "*I fully realize that no wealth or position can long endure unless built upon truth and justice; therefore, I will engage in no transaction that does not benefit all whom it affects.*" Truth and justice are godly principles to follow.

To help me pursue my passion to paint and write full time, I bought John C. Maxwell's book *Put Your Dream to the Test* and carefully followed his guidelines to determine whether my pursuit was not only godly but ready to be tested. I wanted to know what I was doing and why (see Luke 6:46–49). I wanted to do the Father's will and not just pursue works (see Matthew 7:21–23). I created a detailed plan, a vision with steps and goals that can be measured, of where I wanted to go. I wrote it down (see Habakkuk 2:2). I mapped out a course and set sail on a new sea! I review my plan with my wife and others and continually update it using their counsel and the Lord to help lead me. With my plan identified, I am better able to cut activities that do not support or contribute to the accomplishment of my goals.

Then the LORD answered me and said: "Write the vision and make it plain on tablets, that he may run who reads it. For the vision is yet for an appointed time; but at the end it will speak, and it will not lie. Though it tarries, wait for it; because it will surely come, it will not tarry."

Habakkuk 2:2–3

12. Practice Patience

To everything there is a season, a time for every purpose under heaven…

Ecclesiastes 3:1

1 Corinthians 14:40 says, *"Let all things be done decently and in order."* In Luke 12:42, *"And the Lord said, "Who then is that faithful and wise steward, whom his master will make ruler over his household, to give them their portion of food in due season?"* God clearly has "times" and "seasons." Submit your timing and seasons to Christ.

Again, Proverbs 24:27 tells us to *"Prepare your outside work, make it fit for yourself in the field..."* In other words, develop yourself for work. Make yourself fit or capable to do the work. Success comes when opportunity meets preparedness. Preparation time is not wasted time. Making changes to overcome your circumstances or creating new positive routines that sail you closer to your destination is a journey. It is a process of preparation that takes time and patience.

As you read in chapter 6, Joseph's stories regarding his brothers and the Pharaoh (see Genesis 37–50) are the epitome of setbacks or circumstances that were difficult to overcome. Imagine being told in a dream about the greatness you will experience and then going through years of betrayal, enslavement, false accusations, imprisonment, and such before realizing your dream. Yet Joseph remained faithful and righteous. Not only did his brothers bow down to him, but Joseph's master (the Lord) made him second in command of all Egypt.

Desiring things before their due season or proper timing is a form of greed. Ask yourself why you want something? Ask whether you are using the wrong means to get there. What you want and how you get it must be justified *and* in harmony with God to be blessed. Matthew 25:21 tells us that we must be *"...faithful with a few things..."* to be *"...ruler over many things."* We must *keep* our delight in the Lord to receive the desires of our hearts.

When the Jews entered the Promised Land, there were battles to take dominion and territory, and they had to overcome giants. As you sail into your promised land, you too will likely have high seas and sea monsters to overcome. During your journey make your production glorify the God. Luke 6:45 says *"A good man out of the good treasure of his heart brings forth good; and an evil man out of the evil treasure of his heart brings forth evil. For out of the abundance of the heart his mouth speaks."* Does your mouth and production glorify God?

Do not be gullible! Use discernment to make decisions that guard your heart to remain righteous. Proverbs 13:11 says, *"Wealth gained by dishonesty will be diminished...."* Guard your boat and supplies (your provisions or means to make a living), guard your cargo (your career or work that produces a harvest), and guard your harvest (your savings and assets that work for you and eventually allow you to retire). Be a good steward of what you already have. Learn basic accounting: Proverbs 27:23–24 says to *"Be diligent to know the state of your flocks, and attend to your herds; for riches are not forever, nor does a crown endure to all generations."* Self-discipline will keep you from wasting resources—self-control is a gift of the Spirit. (see Proverbs 28:19–20). You grow into self-control. Control the appetites of your flesh. A modest start on a strong but small boat is much better than grand "bon voyage" on a weak cruise ship. Which boat would you prefer to ride?

The soul of the diligent shall be made rich.

Proverbs 13:4

"*He who has a slack hand becomes poor, but the hand of the diligent makes rich.*"

Proverbs 10:4

Chapter 12

God the Gracious Captain

> *And do not be conformed to this world, but be transformed by the renewing of your mind, that you may prove what is that good and acceptable and perfect will of God.*
>
> Romans 12:2

Renewing of Your Mind by Mark Kuhne, commissioned by Tracy Trost, Trost Moving Pictures, depicts the mind's transformation as a butterfly. Hold the image to a mirror and see if you can find the verse.

Best of all, we have an impact on the world when we change ourselves.

Thank goodness Kristin's father kindly brought another fishing boat to the cabin for use that summer—at least I could still fish! (from "The Parable of the Pontoon Boat")

There is a God. It is through our experiences that we know our Father in Heaven who created us. We die to the old, renew the mind, and renovate our thinking by creating new godly routines and goals.

We don't have to live according to our circumstances: Through Joseph, we know that our history does not have to determine our destiny. We can live righteously to overcome circumstances. Best of all, we can have an impact on the world when we change ourselves. Through paintings and writing, my boat will carry light into a dark world. I will have an impact. I am called to greatness.

You are too! What are you called to do? Prepare and do it. An ugly season in your life can be preparation time that teaches you much about yourself. If you have the right motivation and timing, God will turn it into an awesome season of your life. Through my circumstances, I have a much better relationship with Christ. I can hear Him more clearly than ever before. Lay your circumstances at the foot of the cross and ask God to take the helm of your boat. His plans for me are much better than my fleshly plans. I seeded my circumstances and losses into the Kingdom of God and I am reaping a harvest far greater than my expectations.

His power is through us when we carry out the desires of our heart when those desires are in harmony with His. The enemy is already defeated! In the book *Face to Face with God*, Bill Johnson says, *"The devil is a pawn in the hands of the Master—his greatest attempts to destroy are always reworked to bring glory to God and strength to His people"* (see Romans 8:28). My pastors, Dr. Timothy Peterson and Cherrié Peterson, have both taught frequently on Romans (see chapter 13:11–14): *"Wake up (open your eyes and ears so you can see and hear), clean up (cast off what is darkness, build right relationships), behave (build your reputation), and grow up (feed your spirit, not your flesh)"* (see 1 Corinthians 3:1-3) with author notation, which taught me to grow up!).

> The success of your journey is not measured by your words, but by your course and your production or fruit.

Only be strong and very courageous, that you may observe to do according to all the law which Moses My servant commanded you; do not turn from it to the right hand or to the left, that you may prosper wherever you go.

Joshua 1:7

For the eyes of the LORD run to and fro throughout the whole earth, to show Himself strong on behalf of those whose heart is loyal to Him...

2 Chronicles 16:9

The success of your journey is not measured by your words, but by your course and your production or fruit. There is power in the life you live and how it looks to others. To those hurt in the process, it may take a long time for your reputation to be repaired and restored. Some people, even born-again Bible believers may never forgive you. Without realizing it, those who do not forgive are assuming God's role of judgment and want you to be judged according to their own standards. Be careful. God will judge you *as you judge others*. Don't confuse "judging to discern" with "judging to condemn." We are called to discern so we can live righteously. 1 Thessalonians 5:21 tells us to *"test all things; hold fast what is good."* We need to hold everything up to Scripture—the Word is our authority.

> *Judge not, that you be not judged. For with what judgment you judge, you will be judged; and with the measure you use, it will be measured back to you.*
>
> Matthew 7:1–2

> *Judge not, and you shall not be judged. Condemn not, and you shall not be condemned. Forgive, and you will be forgiven.*
>
> Luke 6:37

Have you ever wondered why we suffer? Have you ever wondered why we have tribulations that cause suffering? You understand the wilderness of tribulation and trials, the wilderness where you are tested and tried so you have more power and authority from God flowing through you to build the Kingdom of God after you come out of that wilderness. Beyond that, we question whether God is really God when we or someone we know suffers. Our faith in God can be greatly shaken when we suffer from such an event as physical injuries, severe illnesses, rape, or the death of a loved one. Maybe our faith is put to the test when we see a child suffering from a terminal illness or a parent of several young children given just a few months to live. We ask, "Why God?" If God were really God, if God were all-powerful, why would he allow that?

On one hand the Bible says, *"For this reason many are weak and sick among you, and many sleep. For if we would judge ourselves, we would not be judged. But when we are judged, we are chastened by the Lord, that we may not be condemned with the world"* (1 Corinthians 11:30–32). John MacArthur explains, *"Believers are kept from being consigned to hell, not only by divine decree, but by divine intervention"* (*MacArthur Study Bible*, page 1746). He goes on to say, *"The Lord chastens to drive His people back to righteousness behavior and even sends death to some in the church to remove them before they could be condemned."* You failed at a tribulation or trial and didn't judge yourself.

On the other hand the Bible says, *"Blessed be the God...who comforts us in all our tribulation, that we may be able to comfort those who are in any trouble, with the comfort with which we ourselves are comforted by God"* (2 Corinthians 1:3–4). God's comfort is to build us up and give us strength to walk through the tribulation or suffering. We too are then to be comforters to others.

Of course, we don't run into tribulation or wish to be seriously ill just so we can have power or authority or be edified through God's comfort. You don't need to ask God to "bring it on!" Remember what I said earlier? Be careful for what you ask for, because you just might get it!

In Hebrews 5:8, we learn that Christ, our example to follow, "*... learned obedience by the things which He suffered.*" Christ didn't need to learn obedience any more than he needed to overcome the temptations in the wilderness. Suffering for our sake and temptations confirmed his humanity and allowed him to be the only sacrifice that would overcome all of our sins. We, on the other hand, do need to learn obedience. We are often "dull of hearing" or slow to learn what the gospel teaches us. Through suffering, trials, and temptations, we learn the correct application of the gospel so we may advance spiritually, so we may learn even more and have greater understanding as we mature. If we don't learn from our suffering, trials, and temptations, then we have not profited. Worse, don't be shocked when you face the same suffering, trials and temptations again—sooner or later you will profit.

Sooner or later Christ will get your attention and set you straight. Based on Hebrews 12:8–9, discipline is training, not punishment: God is educating you, which is why you must never drop out. He's treating you as His child. Consider your circumstances as training, a normal experience for children. If God doesn't discipline and train you, then you are not His child. Embrace this training so you truly can live. At the time, training is not much fun, but later it will pay off handsomely. We mature into God's holy best!

For the kingdom of God is not in word but in power.

1 Corinthians 4:20

But thanks be to God, who gives us the victory through our Lord Jesus Christ. Therefore, my beloved brethren, be steadfast, immovable, always abounding in the work of the Lord, knowing that your labor is not in vain in the Lord.

1 Corinthians 15:57–58

We are to let go of distractions and be present with the Lord. Allow the Holy Spirit to shed light on your life and circumstances so you can begin a journey of cleansing, healing, and growth. If you learn just three things from my experiences, learn to fear the Lord your God, learn not to be gullible, and learn to let go of your control in order to submit to God. Psalm 46:10 says, *"Be still, and know that I am God...."*

Give God the helm of your boat!

If you **have** *a personal relationship with Christ Jesus*, but haven't yet fully yielded your heart and life to the Master Mariner, and you are ready to give Him the helm now, let's pray...

Lord Jesus, You are my Captain. I give the helm to my life, my heart, fully over to the desires of Your heart and will. Help me to feel Your presence and to hear Your divine whisper. Lead me. I ask for revelation. Illuminate the waters before me that I may more easily see the journey You have designed for me. Guide me. Shed Your light and countenance upon me. I ask the Holy Spirit to fill me with images and thoughts that teach me about Your Word so I can apply it to my life and journey. Jesus, give me truth! Give me a teachable heart. Give me ears to hear and a heart receptive to Your voice. I yield to You, Lord. Thank You for Your grace and mercy. Open my mind's eye and let me see supernaturally. I ask to be in harmony with Your Spirit, Lord. I soak in Your majestic presence. Despite any mighty waters that may rage against me, I enjoy protection, healing, and restoration. I see the power of the Word in my mind's eye. I see my purpose here on earth from Your point of view. Thank You, Lord, for treasuring me that You covered me with Your blood and forgave me of all my sins. Thank You for giving me a special purpose...a mission! Help me grow and spiritually mature so I can accomplish my purpose. I am Your child. Speak to me. I am ready to hear You, Lord Jesus! Let's sail! Amen.

If you **do not have** *a personal relationship with Christ Jesus*, if you have not yet received Jesus Christ as your Lord and Savior, if you are tired of struggling and floating by on your own strength, if your heart desires the promises of our Lord and Master Mariner and you want Jesus to dwell within you now, let's pray out loud with your lips...

Lord Jesus, here I am. I come to You in prayer. I repent and ask for the forgiveness of my sins. I understand that You will accept me just as I am. I realize that I fall short of the glory of God and need Jesus in my life as my personal Savior. I am tired of living on my strength alone. I confess with my mouth and believe with my heart that Jesus is Your Son, that Jesus died on the cross, and that God raised Jesus from the dead so I can have eternal life in heaven. I ask You right now to receive me as Your child. I open my heart, my eyes, and my ears to You: Come now and dwell in me. Be my personal Lord and Savior. I give You the helm of my life. Thank You for washing away my sins with Your blood. Thank You for forgiving me of all my sins. I will worship and obey You, because Your Word is the truth, the way, and the light. I place all my cares and burdens at the foot of Your cross. I confess that I am born again, a child of God. Thank You for writing my name in the Lamb's Book of Life. Let's set sail. In Jesus' name, Amen.

Benediction

May your seas be calm. May the wind against your sails glide you towards your destiny, the destiny designed just for you by our Father, God. By day and by night, may His light and face shine upon you and be gracious to you. May your harvest be plentiful. May His glory rise upon you…

For it is the God who commanded light to shine out of darkness, who has shone in our hearts to give the light of the knowledge of the glory of God in the face of Jesus Christ.

2 Corinthians 4:6

Instead of mighty waves bearing down against the bow of your soul, may His supernatural light shine and lift up your soul!

You are blessed. Go now and bless others.

Afterword

> *Forgetting those things which are behind, and reaching forth unto those things which are ahead.*
>
> Philippians 3:13

Well, here it is, the book we talked about many times while sitting in my living room. We laughed, we cried, and most of all, we overcame and learned.

I remember the Lord speaking to me in the midst of one of our adversities—"Lies will always die and the truth will always live." Outlive the lie and people will know the truth! This is exactly what Mark and Kristin did: You outlived the lie and it had to die.

One of my favorite "locating" scriptures is Proverbs 24:10: *"If you faint in the day of adversity, Your strength is small."*

I'm a firm believer that adversity makes the strong stronger! Mark and Kristin, watching you walk through this storm together only confirms for me how strong the two of you are in Christ.

I especially found myself thinking of how young people who tend to be so trustworthy and eager need to be "warned" of the "bullies" or "Jesses" in life. Thank you, thank you, for sharing your story in ink so generations to come can learn too.

On another occasion the Lord said to me, "Trustworthy people trust people, and dysfunctional people destroy people." The trustworthy can become prey for the dysfunctional. That's exactly what happened to you! Because you and Kristin are trustworthy, the dysfunctional took advantage of it.

Lastly, I'm so glad you sailed through to calmer seas! Your book *had* to be written. Thank you for reliving this pain in your past so others can learn from your experiences and avoid raging waters bearing down on their souls! *"**Giving God the Helm: Overcoming Storms of Adversity**"* will be in my self-helps reach for all those who need to be ready to identify the unreasonable people and situations in life.

—Cherrié Peterson, pastor, counselor
Christ Family Church International,
Christian Family Church World Outreach

Bible Verse Affirmations

From chapter 11, you learned to immerse yourself in affirmations, music, books, DVDs, teaching CDs, and such. I'll say it again: Enough cannot be said about writing down affirmations and repeating them regularly. Repeat positive affirmations and seed your mind, soul, and spirit. Seeds grow.

To help you, here is a list of numerous Scriptures (in no particular order) that Kristin and I have found useful. Consider choosing several from this list and adding several more that are special to you and read them daily.

Kristin and I take affirmations a step further: We not only print and read them but also take turns reading them together aloud and using a digital recorder to record and load the reading on our MP3 players. (When I say we take turns, well, we went overboard: After reading through the first time, we immediately switched and read them again a second time. In other words, we each read every verse at least once.) Why wait for your ship to come in? Start seeding your mind now. What are you waiting for?

Although our recording is not word-for-word as written in the Bible (or below), if you wish to have a free copy of our digital recording, e-mail me at info@OvercomingForLife.com to request "Mark and Kristin's Affirmations MP3" and provide your first and last name and your e-mail address. If you would, please tell me what you think of this book *Giving **God the Helm: Overcoming Storms of Adversity***. What difference is it making in your life? I would love to hear your story! And Kristin and I welcome any suggestions you have for improvements or for additional workbooks or other topics to address—thanks!

Now it shall come to pass, if you diligently obey the voice of the LORD your God, to observe carefully all His commandments which I command you today, that the LORD your God will set you high above all nations of the earth. And all these blessings shall come upon you and overtake you, because you obey the voice of the LORD your God: blessed shall you be in the city, and blessed shall you be in the country. Blessed shall be the fruit of your body, the produce of your ground and the increase of your herds, the increase of your cattle and the offspring of your flocks. Blessed shall be your basket and your kneading bowl. Blessed shall you be when you come in, and blessed shall you be when you go out. The LORD will cause your enemies who rise against you to be defeated before your face; they shall come out against you one way and flee before you seven ways. The LORD will command the blessing on you in your storehouses and in all to which you set your hand, and He will bless you in the land which the LORD your God is giving you.

The LORD will establish you as a holy people to Himself, just as He has sworn to you, if you keep the commandments of the LORD your God and walk in His ways. Then all peoples of the earth shall see that you are called by the name of the LORD, and they shall be afraid of you. And the LORD will grant you plenty of goods, in the fruit of your body, in the increase of your livestock, and in the produce of your ground, in the land of which the LORD swore to your fathers to give you. The LORD will open to you His good treasure, the heavens, to give the rain to your land in its season, and to bless all the work of your hand. You shall lend to many nations, but you shall not borrow. And the LORD will make you the head and not the tail; you shall be above only, and not be beneath, if you heed the command-ments of the LORD your God, which I command you today, and are careful to observe them. So you shall not turn aside from any of the words which I command you this day, to the right or the left, to go after other gods to serve them. Deuteronomy 28:1–9

And He will love you and bless you and multiply you; He will also bless the fruit of your womb and the fruit of your land, your grain and your new wine and your oil, the increase of your cattle and the offspring of your flock, in the land of which He swore to your fathers to give you. Deuteronomy 7:13

The LORD your God will make you abound in all the work of your hand, in the fruit of your body, in the increase of your livestock, and in the produce of your land for good. For the LORD will again rejoice over you for good as He rejoiced over your fathers. Deuteronomy 30:9

Let the peoples praise You, O God; let all the peoples praise You. Then the earth shall yield her increase; God, our own God, shall bless us. God shall bless us, And all the ends of the earth shall fear Him. Psalm 67:5–7

You shall increase my greatness, and comfort me on every side. Psalm 71:21

Yes, the LORD will give what is good; and our land will yield its increase. Psalm 85:12

May the LORD give you increase more and more, you and your children. Psalm 115:14

Honor the LORD with your possessions, and with the first fruits of all your increase; so your barns will be filled with plenty, and your vats will overflow with new wine. Proverbs 3:9–10

…he who gathers by labor will increase. Proverbs 13:11

The wisdom of the prudent is to understand his way. Proverbs 14:8

The wise woman builds her house. Proverbs 14:1

Then He will give the rain for your seed with which you sow the ground, and bread of the increase of the earth; it will be fat and plentiful. Isaiah 30:23

Now may He who supplies seed to the sower, and bread for food, supply and multiply the seed you have sown and increase the fruits of your righteousness. 2 Corinthians 9:10

The man began to prosper, and continued prospering until he became very prosperous; for he had possessions of flocks and possessions of herds and a great number of servants. Genesis 26:13–14

…that the blessing of Abraham might come upon the Gentiles in Christ Jesus… Galatians 3:14

And his master saw that the LORD was with him and that the LORD made all he did to prosper in his hand. Genesis 39:3

Therefore keep the words of this covenant, and do them, that you may prosper in all that you do. Deuteronomy 29:9

Then the LORD your God will bring you to the land which your fathers possessed, and you shall possess it. He will prosper you and multiply you more than your fathers. Deuteronomy 30:5

...And as long as he sought the LORD, God made him prosper. 2 Chronicles 26:5

And in every work that he began in the service of the house of God, in the law and in the commandment, to seek his God, he did it with all his heart. So he prospered. 2 Chronicles 31:21

He shall be like a tree planted by the rivers of water, that brings forth its fruit in its season, whose leaf also shall not wither; and whatever he does shall prosper. Psalm 1:3

Who is the man that fears the LORD? Him shall He teach in the way He chooses. He himself shall dwell in prosperity, and his descendants shall inherit the earth. Psalm 25:12–13

...let the LORD be magnified, Who has pleasure in the prosperity of His servant. Psalm 35:27

...he who trusts in the LORD will be prospered. Proverbs 28:25

For when God made a promise to Abraham, because He could swear by no one greater, He swore by Himself, saying, "Surely blessing I will bless you, and multiplying I will multiply you." And so, after he had patiently endured, he obtained the promise. Hebrews 6:13–15

The righteous will flourish like foliage. Proverbs 11:28

The blessing of the LORD makes one rich, and He adds no sorrow with it.
Proverbs 10:22

That I may cause those who love me to inherit wealth, that I may fill their treasuries. Proverbs 8:21

The LORD God is a sun and shield; the LORD will give grace and glory; no good thing will He withhold from those who walk uprightly. Psalm 84:11–12

So Jesus answered and said, "Assuredly, I say to you, there is no one who has left house or brothers or sisters or father or mother or wife or children or lands, for My sake and the gospel's, who shall not receive a hundredfold now in this time… Mark 10:29–30

Beloved, I pray that you may prosper in all things and be in health, just as your soul prospers. 3 John 2

For you know the grace of our Lord Jesus Christ, that though He was rich, yet for your sakes He became poor, that you through His poverty might become rich. 2 Corinthians 8:9

And my God shall supply all your need according to His riches in glory by Christ Jesus. Philippians 4:19

A good man leaves an inheritance to his children's children, but the wealth of the sinner is stored up for the righteous. Proverbs 13:22

Honor the LORD with your possessions, and with your firstfruits of all your increase; So your barns will be filled with plenty, and your vats will overflow with new wine. Proverbs 3:9–10

If they obey and serve Him, they shall spend their days in prosperity, and their years in pleasures. Job 36:11

Give, and it will be given to you: good measure, pressed down, shaken together, and running over will be put into your bosom. For with the same measure that you use, it will be measured back to you. Luke 6:38

Praise the LORD! Blessed is the man who fears the LORD, who delights greatly in His commandments. His descendants will be mighty on earth; the generation of the upright will be blessed. Wealth and riches will be in his house, and his righteousness endures forever. Psalms 112:1–3

"Bring all the tithes into the storehouse, that there may be food in My house, and try Me now in this," says the LORD of hosts, "If I will not open for you the windows of heaven and pour out for you such blessing that there will not be room enough to receive it. And I will rebuke the devourer for your sakes, so that he will not destroy the fruit of your ground, nor shall the vine fail to bear fruit for you in the field," says the LORD of hosts; and all nations will call you blessed, for you will be a delightful land," says the LORD of hosts. Malachi 3:10–12

… you were faithful over a few things, I will make you ruler over many things… Matthew 25:21

… whatever things are true, whatever things are noble, whatever things are just, whatever things are pure, whatever things are lovely, whatever things are

of good report, if there is any virtue and if there is anything praiseworthy—meditate on these things. Philippians 4:8

A wise man will hear and increase learning, and a man of understanding will attain wise counsel. Proverbs 1:5

There remains therefore a rest for the people of God. Hebrews 4:9

Though I walk in the midst of trouble, You will revive me; You will stretch out Your hand against my enemies, and Your right hand will save me. Psalm 138:7

I press toward the goal… Philippians 3:14

…choose life, that both you and your descendents may live. Deuteronomy 30:19

Therefore gird up the loins of your mind, be sober, and rest your hope fully upon the grace that is to be brought to you … 1 Peter 1:13

…forgetting those things which are behind and reaching forward to those things which are ahead. Philippians 3:13

…exhort one another daily… Hebrews 3:13

…comfort each other and edify one another… 1 Thessalonians 5:11

… nothing will be impossible for you. Matthew 17:20

For as he thinks in his heart, so is he… Proverbs 23:7

…walk circumspectly, not as fools but as wise, redeeming the time… Ephesians 5:16

Every branch in Me that does not bear fruit He takes away; and every branch that bears fruit He prunes, that it may bear more fruit. John 15:2

...write the vision, and make it plain... Habakkuk 2:2

Discretion will preserve you, and understanding will keep you. Proverbs 2:11

A word fitly spoken is like apples of gold in settings of silver. Proverbs 25:11

If you extend your soul to the hungry and satisfy the afflicted soul, then your light shall dawn in the darkness, and your darkness shall be as noonday. Isaiah 58:10

Wise people store up knowledge... Proverbs 10:14

...be thankful. Colossians 3:15

Let all things be done decently and in order. 1 Corinthians 14:40

Create in me a clean heart, O God... Psalm 51:10

Go to the ant, you sluggard! Consider her ways and be wise...Provides her supplies in the summer, and gathers her food in the harvest. Proverbs 6:6, 8

Though I walk through the valley of the shadow of death, I will fear no evil: for you art with me... Psalm 23:4

...I am God, and there is none like Me, declaring the end from the beginning... Isaiah 46:9-10

... *"I am the LORD your God, who teaches you to profit,"*... Isaiah 48:17

...*we are well able to overcome it.* Numbers 13:30

Be strong and do not let your hands be weak, for your work will be rewarded. 2 Chronicles 15:7

The generous soul will be made rich, and he who waters will also be watered himself. Proverbs 11:25

...*do not turn from it to the right hand or to the left, that you may prosper wherever you go.* Joshua 1:7

I will give you the treasures of darkness and hidden riches of secret places... Isaiah 45:3

But others fell on good ground and yielded a crop: some a hundredfold, some sixty, some thirty. Matthew 13:8

The righteous man walks in his integrity; his children are blessed after him. Proverbs 20:7

... *those who deal truthfully are His delight.* Proverbs 12:22

...*I follow what is good.* Psalm 38:20

...*let us run with endurance the race that is set before us.* Hebrews 12:1

...*I will not leave you nor forsake you.* Joshua 1:5

...*the soul of the diligent shall be made rich.* Proverbs 13:4

The fruit of the Spirit is love, joy, peace, longsuffering, kindness, goodness, faithfulness, gentleness, and self control... Galatians 5:22–23

Cast your bread upon the waters, for you will find it after many days. Ecclesiastes 11:1

...Guard what was committed to your trust... 1 Timothy 6:20

...men always ought to pray and not lose heart... Luke 18:1

Then Elijah said to Ahab, "Go up, eat and drink; for there is the sound of abundance of rain." 1 Kings 18:41

I will make them and the places all around My hill a blessing; and I will cause showers to come down in their season; there shall be showers of blessing. Then the trees of the field shall yield their fruit, and the earth shall yield her increase. They shall be safe in their land; and they shall know that I am the Lord, when I have broken the bands of their yoke and delivered them from the hand of those who enslaved them. Ezekiel 34:26–27

Additional Resources

Nigel Allan, *The Key to Life, Born a Winner, Live a Winner, Die a Winner,* ATS–Publishers, 2004.

Dr. C. Thomas Anderson, *Becoming a Millionaire God's Way,* Winword Publishing, 2004.

John Belt, *Overcomers, To Him Who Overcomes* (instrumental, audio CD), Live In His Presence Productions, 2007.

John Bevere, *Fear of the Lord,* Charisma House, A Strang Company, 1997, 2006.

John Bevere, *Driven by Eternity Devotional Workbook,* Messenger International, 2006.

Michael Cameneti, *The Missing Ingredient to Success,* Faith Library Publications, 2004.

Steven M.R. Covey, *The Speed of Trust, The One Thing That Changes Everything,* Free Press, 2006.

Rev. Chris D'Amico, "Just Don't Give Up, Don't Quit," Guest Speaker, Christ's Family Church International, www.chrisdamicoministries.org.

Mike Francen, *Destiny*, Francen World Outreach Publications, 2001.

Malcolm Gladwell, *Blink: The Power of Thinking Without Thinking*, Little, Brown and Company, 2005.

Malcolm Gladwell, *The Tipping Point: How Little Things Can Make a Big Difference*, Back Bay Books, 2002.

Mark Gungor, "Laugh Your Way to a Better Marriage" DVD, release date January 12, 2009, including "The Flag Page" measures of passion, www.laughyourway.com/what-motivates-you.

Bob Harrison, Increase Events, three- to five-day seminars, www.Increase.org.

Bob Harrison, *Power Points For Success*, Whitaker House, 2005.

Bob Harrison, *Strategies for Success* (audio CD), Harrison International Seminars, 2000.

Bob Harrison, *7 Habits of Highly Successful Palm Trees* (audio CD), Harrison International Seminars.

Napoleon Hill, *Think & Grow Rich* (CD set), Ballentine Books, 1987.

John Paul Jackson, *Unmasking the Jezebel Spirit*, Streams Publications, 2002.

Bill Johnson, *Face to Face with God*, Charisma House, 2007.

Kolbe A Index assessment of "instinctive method of operation (MO)" www.kolbe.com/assessmentTools/assessment-tools.cfm.

Brian Klemmer, "Champions' Workshop" and "Personal Mastery" seminar, www.Klemmer.com.

Brian Klemmer, *If How To's Were Enough We Would All Be Skinny, Rich and Happy*, Klemmer & Associates, 2000.

Brian Klemmer, *When Good Intentions Run Smack Into Reality: Twelve Lessons to Coach Yourself and Others to Peak Performance*, Insight Publishing Group, 2004.

Brian Klemmer, *Eating the Elephant One Bite At a Time*, VIP, 2006.

Brian Klemmer, *The Pursuit and Practice of Personal Mastery: Unique Perspectives and Timeless Principles* (audio cassettes), Klemmer & Associates, 1999.

Kristin Kuhne, *Expect a Miracle* (audio CD), Overcoming For Life LLC, 2010, www.OvercomingForLife.com.

Kristin Kuhne, *Rahab and Me* (audio CD), Overcoming For Life LLC, 2010, www.OvercomingForLife.com.

Kristin Kuhne, *Your Circumstances Don't Define You* (audio CD), Overcoming For Life LLC, 2010, www.OvercomingForLife.com.

John MacArthur, *The MacArthur Study Bible*, Word Publishing, 1997.

John C. Maxwell, *Put Your Dream to the Test: 10 Questions to Help You See It and Seize It*, Thomas Nelson, 2009.

Ned Miller, "Sales Leadership in Turbulent Times, Rituals to Drive Change" MZ Bierly e-news article, *Sales Management Matters*, Volume 4, issue 2, February 17, 2009, www.mzbierlyconsulting. com.

Myers-Briggs Type Indicator (MBTI) personality inventory exercise, www.myersbriggs.org/my-mbti-personality-type/mbti-basics.

Dr. Timothy V. Peterson, *What You See is What You Get!* (audio CD), Christ's Family Church International, 2010.

Michael Q. Pink, "The Raincatcher's Secret: 7 Ancient Paths to Wealth, Wisdom & the Wonder of God" (audio CD: *Selling Among Wolves—Without Joining the Pack!*), www.sellingamong-wolves.net/raincatcher.

Michael Q. Pink, "Vision: Getting it Right, Seeing it Clearly & Following Through" (audio CD: *Selling Among Wolves—Without Joining the Pack!*), www.sellingamongwolves.net/raincatcher.

Larry Randolf, *User Friendly Prophecy*, Destiny Image Publishers, 1998.

Eddie Rasnake, *Using Your Spiritual Gifts*, AMG Publishers, 2005.

Tom Rath, *Strengths Finder 2.0*, Gallup Press, 2007, see also www. strengthsfinder.com.

Vassula Ryden, "Beware the Jezebel Spirit," True Life in God web site, December 2004, www.tlig.org/en/spirituality/letters/jezebel.

Benjamin Smith, *I Hear a Sound of Abundance!* Guest speaker, Strawberry Lake Christian Retreat and Conference Center, September 1, 2007, www.prophetbensmith.org.

Matt Sorger, Matt Sorger Ministries, 2008 podcast "Go into Your Wilderness!" www.mattsorger.com, www.resourcesforchristians.net/music/Podcasts/MATT%20SORGER%20-%20 AUDIO%20PODCAST.

About the Author

Now faith is the substance of things hoped for, the evidence of things not seen.

Hebrews 11:1

Trust in the LORD with all your heart and lean not on your own understanding; in all your ways acknowledge him, and he will make your paths straight.

Proverbs 3:5–6

Mark Kuhne has more than twenty-five years of experience in commercial banking; he has advised and financed entrepreneurs in various industries.

Born in 1956, he began drawing at an early age. As early as elementary school, his drawings and paintings were placed in community art shows and he won art awards every year he attended Redlands High School in California.

Hanging with the wrong crowd, Mark knew he had to leave Redlands and give up a four-year art scholarship at Redlands

University. Besides, his father had said, "No son of mine is going to make money painting." Mark believed him, gave up his dream to paint, moved to Minnesota, and obtained a BA degree in economics from the University of Minnesota and an MBA in finance from the University of St. Thomas, St. Paul, Minnesota. Mark knows firsthand how powerful parents' words are, so he encourages his four children and others to follow their dreams.

One early morning in August 2007, Mark wasn't quite sleeping but felt someone "touch" him. Turning, he saw no one, and immediately believed that it was the Holy Spirit…but why? A week later at a Christian retreat, his family listened to Prophet Benjamin Smith preach "I hear a sound of abundance!" from 1 Kings 18:41–46 in which Elijah says to Ahab, *"…there is the sound of abundance of rain…"* In late September, Mark dreamed he was driving on a highway with a wheat field to his left undulating in the wind like waves in a sea. The horizon was dark and ready to rain. The wheat was golden and bending over from the weight of the "fruit." Golden light was shining upon the wheat. The light was Christ, the harvest was near, and the rain was God pouring out His blessings!

Within a few days, the Lord prompted him to "paint that dream." Mark thought the Lord was crazy. Like most children when asked to do something they think is above their abilities, he questioned the request: "I haven't had oils, brushes, and palette knives for at least twenty-five years! Why me? Why now? Can't I wait until I am really old to resume painting? How am I going to do this?"…

and so it went. Finally, Mark relented: "Okay, but if I am going to paint, You [the Holy Spirit] better be painting through me, because I have better things to do than spend a lot of money just to paint something no one except my mother wants!"

God is wonderful! Today, Mark's paintings are inspired by God and based on God's Word. Painting creates opportunities to speak into others as a silent witness and opens doors that otherwise would be closed. Looking back to the "*touch*," Mark believes that the Holy Spirit imparted a renewed gift of painting upon him, an anointing to reach people through his paintings. His dream to paint was reborn.

In July 2010, Mark left his position as Community Bank President to pursue painting and writing full-time. Mark and his wife Kristin sold their cabin in northern Minnesota in August and on the first of September, they moved to American Samoa with the two youngest of their four children (the two oldest are already out on their own). During their stay in American Samoa, Mark finished this book and painted a series of seven paintings titled *The Voice of the Turtle Is Heard* based on Genesis 1:20–22. Mark started another series titled *Monsters and Fools of the Bible*.

This series and other paintings by Mark Kuhne are based on Scripture and can be found at www.KuhneGallery.com. (Contact info@KuhneGallery.com regarding the availability of prints and giclées.)

Sound of Abundance (1 Kings 18:4)

Christ Yielded up His Spirit (Matthew 27:45, 50)

Like a Tree Planted by Rivers of Water (Psalm 1:1–3)

My Hill is a Blessing (Ezekiel 34:26–27)

Praise the Lord (Sun Moon Stars) (Psalm 148:1–4)

Tree of Life (Proverbs 11:30)

Make Disciples (Matthew 28:19)

Door of Hope (Hosea 2:14–23)

Jesus of Galilee (a montage: Matthew 3:13, 16; John 13:12, 14; John 13:4; Acts 1:7–9)

Flourish Like a Palm Tree (Psalm 92:12)

Transformed by the Renewing of Your Mind (Romans 12:2)

The Voice of the Turtle is Heard (seven paintings based on Genesis 1:20–22)

Jezebel and Ahab (1 Kings 21:15, 25)

King Cobra (Psalm 58:4-5; Job 20:12–14; and Jeremiah 8:17)

The Immoral Woman (Proverbs 5:1–23)
King Nebuchadnezzar 1 (Daniel 3:16–23)
King Nebuchadnezzar 2 (Daniel 4:28–33)
Leviathan (Job 41:1–34)

Painting has evolved into Overcoming For Life. Together, Mark and Kristin Kuhne speak and teach and plan to author books, devotional workbooks, meditation booklets and DVDs, CDs, educational curricula, and more, which will be available on the website www.OvercomingForLife.com.

Their first DVD is called *Tree of Life, A Contemplative Prayer.* This DVD is about resting in the Lord's presence, focusing on the Lord, and listening to the Lord. Think of Mark as your tour guide and the image of his painting *Tree of Life* as the starting point of your journey. From there, you let the Holy Spirit lead and show you His way. As you meditate, the Holy Spirit will take over and fill you with images, thoughts, and more.

Mark and Kristin share the mission to improve the lives of people, to reach souls for Christ across the world, to introduce people to a better way of thinking that is founded on proven Biblical principles, and for you to enjoy "increase" in all areas of your life, a life of true prosperity.

About the "Overcoming For Life" Logo

The Sea Turtle

On the shell, the inner portion represents the Father: Our Father in heaven—Creator of the heavens and earth—is represented by the waves (see Genesis 1:1-9). The Son is represented by the cross and is our center of our focus and the power of God (see 1 Corinthians 1:18). The Holy Spirit is represented by the ring, a covenant we have with our Lord.

The turtle's head and tail together represent the sword of the Spirit which is the Word of God (see Ephesians 6:17). The head and upper portions of the front legs are the sword's handle and guard. The tail is the tip of the blade.

The front and rear legs also form the shield of faith (Ephesians 6:14–16): *"...above all, taking the shield of faith with which you will be able to quench all the fiery darts of the wicked one."* We are also to gird our *"...waist with truth, having put on the breastplate of righteousness..."* and shod our feet with the *"preparation of the gospel of peace."*

Sea turtles are peaceful creatures of God, but turtles also wear their armor at all times for protection against predators. Likewise, we too should *"...take up the whole armor of God...having done all, to stand"* (see Ephesians 6:13).

In Samoan folklore, sea turtles are believed to have the power to save fishermen who are lost at sea by bringing them safely to shore. Many today, even believers, are lost in storms of adversity.

Mark and Kristin pray that his paintings, their writings, and their messages will inspire and encourage you and bring you to a higher rock! They pray that you will give God the helm of your life and allow God to fully and completely lead you on your journey through mighty waters.

From the end of the earth I will cry to You, when my heart is overwhelmed; lead me to the rock that is higher than I.

Psalm 61:2

Thus says the LORD, who makes a way in the sea and a path through the mighty waters..." Do not remember the former things, nor consider the things of old. Behold, I will do a new thing, now it shall spring forth; shall you not know it? I will even make a road in the wilderness and rivers in the desert."

Isaiah 43:16-19